Undead Cinema: The Essential Zombie Films

Stephen Hoover

Undead Cinema: The Essential Zombie Films

Library of Congress Control Number: 2014903824

Copyright © 2013 by Stephen Hoover

Book design by: Cat Stewart

Cover design by: 2Faced Design

All rights reserved. No part of this book may be used or reproduced in any manner whatsoever including Internet usage, without written permission of the author.

ISBN: 978-1-941084-14-4

Contents

CHAPTER 1: THE BASICS OF THE LIVING DEAD 1
- The Origin Story 5
- What to Expect 7

CHAPTER 2: WHAT IS A ZOMBIE? 9
- To Shoot or Not to Shoot? 9
- To Shoot 10
- Vodou Origins 11
- Weird Fiction and the Zombie 12
- The Contaminated/Diseased Zombie 13
- The Undead 14
- Blending in Vampires 15
- The Infected Zombie 16
- The Bringers of the End 18
- The Survival Fantasy 19

CHAPTER 3: ZOMBIE PHYSIOLOGY: THE ANATOMY OF THE DEAD 23
- Wave After Wave 23
- The Horde 25
- Making Sense of It All 27
- The Physiology of the Actual Reanimated Dead 27
- The Rotting Problem 28
- Fast and Infected: Zombie Variants 29
- The Need for Speed 29
- Escaping the Fast Zombies 30
- The Plague Zombies 31
- The Mutant or Engineered Zombie 34

CHAPTER 4: ZOMBIE PHYSIOLOGY PART II: KILLING A ZOMBIE 37
- Remember the Different Types 37
- Headshot 38
- Decapitation 39
- Kill It With Fire! 40

ZOMBIE KILLERS AND SIGNATURE WEAPONS	40
BOWS AND ARROWS/CROSSBOWS	41
AXES AND TOMAHAWKS	41
MACHETES	42

CHAPTER 5: STORY STRUCTURE 43

SURVIVING THE END	44
POLITICAL DRAMA, AND ZOMBIES	46
CONSUMERISM	49
SCIENTISTS GONE MAD	50
NATURAL DISASTERS AND TERRORISM	51
THE ZOM COM	53

CHAPTER 6: VILLAINS AND HEROES OF THE ZOMBIE APOCALYPSE 55

THE HEROES	55
THE COP/SOLIDER	56
THE SURVIVALIST	56
THE SELF-MOTIVATED	56
THE ALTRUISTIC	57
THE WISE ONE	57
THE INFECTED	57
THE VILLAINS	57
THE VODOU PRIEST	58
THE VODOU PRIEST IN A WHITE LAB COAT	58
MILITARY RUN AMOK	58
HOW THE VODOU PRIEST BECAME A SCIENTIST	58

CHAPTER 7: GREAT DIRECTORS OF THE DEAD 61

GEORGE A. ROMERO	61
THE ROMERO *LIVING DEAD* FILMS AND RATINGS	62
JOHN A. RUSSO	63
PETER JACKSON	63
LUCIO FULCI	63
ZACK SNYDER	64
DANNY BOYLE	64
NOT SLUMMING	64

CHAPTER 8: ZOMBIE FILMS THROUGHOUT THE YEARS ..65

- Dystopia, Mon Amour 66
- The Shifting Natures of Zombies and the Changing Times 67
- Night of the Living Dead: Launching a Legend 67
- Return of the Living Dead: Making Zombies Comical 68
- The 1990s: A Game Changes Everything 71
- The 2000s: The Zombies Get Resurrected 72

CHAPTER 9: "REAL" ZOMBIE INCIDENTS 75

- *Cambodia Has Zombies!* 76
- *British Humor, Again* 76
- *Zombies Mosey Into Cowboy Territory* 77
- *The CDC Recommends Zombie Preparedness* 77
- *Running a Scam with Zombies* 78
- Section II: The Films of the Dead 79
- White Zombie (1932) 81
  - *The Plot* 82
  - *Eerie in the Extreme* 84
  - *The Imperial Angle* 85
  - *What to Watch For* 86
  - *Appreciating These Zombies* 87
- Plan 9 From Outer Space (1959) 89
  - *The Plot* 91
  - *Technology and Its Perils* 94
  - *Space Zombies* 95
  - *Enjoying These Zombies* 98
- The Last Man on Earth (1964) 101
  - *The Plot* 101
  - *Bleaker than Bleak* 103
  - *Enjoying These Zombies* 104
- Night of the Living Dead (1968) 107
  - *The Plot* 108
  - *What Was That?* 110
  - *This Never Happened Before* 111
  - *Enjoying These Zombies* 112
- Horror Express (1972) 115
  - *The Plot* 115

- Another Reason to Explore the Public Domain 118
- Enjoying These Zombies 119

Let Sleeping Corpses Lie (1974) 121
- The Plot 121
- Not Very Well Known, but Very Good 124
- Enjoying These Zombies 126

Dawn of the Dead (1978) 129
- The Plot 129
- Similar to the First, but More Developed 131
- Interesting Themes 133
- The Gore 135
- Enjoying These Zombies 135

Zombi 2 (1979) 137
- The Plot 137
- One of the Best for Gore Fans 139
- Enjoying These Zombies 141

Day of the Dead (1985) 143
- The Plot 143
- An Interesting Twist 146
- Enjoying These Zombies 148

Re-Animator (1985) 151
- The Plot 151
- Really Gory 154
- The Mad Scientist and His Zombies 155
- The Lovecraft Connection 156
- Enjoying These Zombies 157

Return of the Living Dead (1985) 159
- The Plot 159
- Braaaains! 161
- Enjoying These Zombies 162

The Serpent and the Rainbow (1988) 163
- The Plot 163
- Very Eerie 165
- Enjoying These Zombies 166

Dead Alive, AKA Braindead (1992) 169
- The Plot 169
- Beyond Gory 171
- Enjoying These Zombies 172

THE DEAD HATE THE LIVING! (2000) 175
   The Plot 175
   Low-Budget and Derivative 178
   The Zombie Drought 179
   Enjoying These Zombies 180
28 DAYS LATER (2002) 181
   The Plot 181
   Reinventing the Genre 184
   About That Plague 186
   Get the DVD 188
   Enjoying These Zombies 188
RESIDENT EVIL (2002) 191
   The Plot 191
   Good or Not? 193
   The Zombies 194
   Enjoying These Zombies 195
DOOM (2005) 199
   The Plot 199
   So Bad It's Good 201
   The Video Game Element 202
   Enjoying These Zombies 203
DAWN OF THE DEAD (2004) 205
   The Plot 205
   Faster and More Violent 209
   Is It Better than the Original? 211
   Enjoying These Zombies 212
SHAUN OF THE DEAD (2004) 216
   The Plot 216
   A High-End Zom Com 218
   Enjoying These Zombies 219
LAND OF THE DEAD (2005) 221
   The Plot 221
   The Dead Continue to Evolve 223
   The Gore 224
   Enjoying These Zombies 225
FIDO (2006) 227
   The Plot 227
   Not Bad 229

- Enjoying These Zombies 230
- [Rec](2007) 232
  - The Plot 232
  - Overused Idea but Done Well 235
  - The Possession Connection 235
  - Enjoying These Zombies 236
- 28 Weeks Later (2007) 237
  - The Plot 237
  - A Solid Sequel 240
  - Hard Choices 242
  - Enjoying These Zombies 244
- Diary of the Dead (2007) 247
  - The Plot 247
  - Similar, but Different 249
  - Enjoying These Zombies 251
- I Am Legend (2007) 252
  - The Plot 252
  - A Worthy Successor 255
  - Enjoying These Zombies 255
- Survival of the Dead (2009) 257
  - The Plot 257
  - The Final Chapter, as of Now 259
  - Enjoying These Zombies 262
- Zombieland (2009) 265
  - The Plot 265
  - Witty and Grown-Up 267
  - A Great and Funny Guide to Surviving the Zombie Apocalypse 268
  - Enjoying These Zombies 270
- World War Z (2013) 271
  - The Plot 271
  - Familiar, but Fun, Zombies 275
  - What Is Different 276
  - Enjoying These Zombies 277
- Further Recommendations 279
  - The Astro Zombies (1968) 279
  - Zombie Holocaust (1979) 279
  - City of the Dead (1980) 280
  - Zombie High (1987) 280

Return of the Living Dead Part II (1988) 280
Chopper Chicks in Zombietown (1989) 280
Pet Semetary (1989) 281
Bride of Re-Animator (1990) 281
Beyond Re-Animator (2003) 282
Zombie Strippers (2008) 282
Tokyo Zombie (2009) 282
CONCLUSION 283
SOURCES CITED 285

Intro

Zombies are everywhere these days. They're in films, video games, newspaper articles, on television and certainly in the popular imagination. What is it about these creatures that is so compelling? It depends upon which type of zombie you are talking about.

Traditional zombies are the creations of Vodou priests, who use supernatural powers to control the undead. However, the zombies that appear in modern films are more along the lines of ghouls, feeding on dead flesh and killing the living.

However they appear, zombies have garnered themselves a significant place in modern mythology.

This book explores the essential zombie films, with plenty of meaty content on the storylines and stellar elements within the genre. Be aware that not all zombie films are good. In fact, some of them are downright awful. The ones featured in this book, however, are excellent choices for those who want to explore and better understand the zombie genre.

The first chapter gives insight into what zombies are, their folklore origins, and where they seem to be headed. Also discussed are some of the most common tropes that you'll find in zombie films. Knowledge of these recurring themes is vital to appreciating this genre.

Zombie films are oftentimes survival stories, so the characters and story arc can be just as compelling as the monsters themselves. Some directors, notably Romero, have managed to use this genre for serious social commentary.

Whether it's a film that pokes fun at consumerism in a gory way, or a film that just has a good time with the common themes in zombie films, you'll find the best of the best here. Remember that there's always more to explore. A section on some notable directors in the genre is given to help you find good selections beyond what we feature in-depth.

With that being said, board up the windows, turn off the lights and don't make any noise, because the undead seem to be out there in greater numbers than ever these days, and it won't take them 20 minutes to cross your front lawn anymore. From the slow, shambling zombies of the past to the sprinting zombies of today, this book will let you in on why people love these flesh-eating monsters so much!

Chapter 1

The Basics of the Living Dead

Note: The Haitian spelling of the word Voodoo, Vodou, is used in the following text, owing to the largely Haitian origins of traditional zombie myths as they are portrayed in some films.

In 1968, George A. Romero's *Night of the Living Dead* debuted. Theatergoers of the time were presented with an entirely new type of film and, despite its low-budget trappings, upon its release, *Night of the Living Dead (NOTLD)* terrified audiences. Most of the crowd that showed up to see it had apparently expected another of the tamer horror films to which they had become accustomed during the 1950s and early 1960s. *NOTLD* was certainly not that.

NOTLD was a film that utilized grown-up fears to achieve its effect. It may have been low-budget, but the filming style, the feeling of paranoia that pervades the film, and the protagonists' complete confusion, gave the audience an experience of utter helplessness. It is exceptionally gory—particularly for the era—and seems to delight in making the audience feel afraid, uneasy and, sometimes, making them jump out of their seats.

The film spawned an entire genre, and gave birth to one of the most distinctive antagonists in film history: the flesh-eating zombie. In 1968, hell ran out of room, the dead started to walk the earth, and cinema would never be the same again.

Never Saw It Coming

When reviewing *NOTLD*, film critic Roger Ebert concentrated on audience reactions. Those reactions were dramatic. At the showing Ebert attended, many of the attendees were teenagers who had no idea what they were about to see. They were shocked by what took place on-screen. Looking back, it's easy to see why that audience was terrified.

While the 1950s and 1960s had plenty of horror fare, most of it was relatively predictable and safe. The good guys won in the end, and there was perhaps a question mark at the end of the film, or a fleeting shot of the bad guy, to let the audience know that there could be a sequel. Watching the horror films of those days, one would walk away from the end credits with a feeling of satisfaction. The roller coaster was over, the platform where it ended was safe and stable and the audience would on with their lives, one thrill richer for having taken the ride.

NOTLD didn't just break with this tradition; it set it on fire and left it in a burning heap on the lawn of an abandoned farmhouse. It was the first night of an apocalypse that would rock the cinematic world. In *NOTLD*, there is no happy ending; it's darker than darkfrom beginning to end. It never lets up, even for a minute, and it betrays the audience by killing off the most likeable character in a most senseless way.The protagonist, Ben, fights valiantly to save himself and everyone else in the house, but dies due to a shot fired in error by a group of men cleaning up the aftermath of the zombie attacks. There's no resolution.

Chapter 1: Basics of the Living Dead

Ben is a relatable hero and one of the few black heroes in films of the time, making him even more of a standout character. He's cool under pressure, a creative and capable fighter, and does his best to look after everyone's wellbeing, even when they're panicking and paranoid. A nice young couple, who may have rode off to safety with Ben in a more conventional film of the time, end up getting devoured.

This begs the question, of course, as to why this film became so popular that it launched an entire genre of films, books, television shows, and video games. Examining this film in th broadest sense provides some interesting perspectives on what makes these films, and their shambling antagonists, work.

The Paranoia

NOTLD sets itself up as a conventional horror story. A brother and sister go to a cemetery to visit a grave, apparently far from the city. The brother teases the sister, plays on her fears, and utters one of the most memorable movie lines in history:

"They're coming to get you, Barbara."

He does it in an over-the-top movie-villain voice, similar to the horror hosts that were popular on television at that time, but this is a mislead

Soon after Johnny torments Barbara, a zombie dashes out his brains. Even at this point, it's not revealed that the man who kills Johnny is a walking corpse. Soon enough, however, there are hints. The graveyard has plenty of listless, wandering forms—but once they see Barbara, they take on the determination of hungry predators.

A farmhouse proves to be Barbara's only shelter, but there are corpses hidden in the upper floors. A lone man trying to protect himself against the onslaught is her only company.

The media doesn't know what's going on and the best advice that the sheriff can give is to shoot the creatures in the head. No one knows

Chapter 2: What Is a Zombie?

people how to build a zombie survival kit. The CDC even picked up on this, issuing zombie survival instructions that serve equally as well as instructions on how to survive any natural disaster. The CDC doesn't currently recommend obtaining a shotgun or a machete, however, though this is the case for the sites and books that take the matter less seriously.

Why would an fictional scenario work for emergencies as well as actual survival instructions? Again, because this scenario plays on real-life fears. While they may be on much smaller scales, riots, terrorist attacks, disease outbreaks, natural disasters, and other catastrophes can closely parallel the nature of fictional zombie attacks. People need to have food, water, transportation, an escape plan, means of communication, medication, and tools to help them survive.

Horror films take genuinely scary scenarios and allow the audience to experience them without putting themselves in harm's way. In the case of zombie films, particularly those that play into modern fears, we get to watch society collapse without having to lose any of what it has to offer. When we go home after the movie, the lights still turn on, the water still runs, and our neighbors aren't trying to steal our supplies or eat us. For the runtime of the film, however, we get to enjoy a sort of roller coaster ride that takes us through some of our most significant and widely shared anxieties.

The Survival Fantasy

Part of the fantasy of zombie films is the idea of survival. In these films, the group of survivors tends to have enough weapons, food, and other supplies to endure for a long time. In reality, the weight of the water one human being needs to survive for even a week is a great deal to carry.

In some cases, the filmmakers avoid getting too farfetched by having the main characters join up with people who would be equipped for hardship, such as military units or survivalists. In some cases, even

machete. The zombies come in great numbers, so there's always plenty of cannon fodder for the protagonists to chew up, too.

Zombies endure, in many regards, because they are perfect horror film villains. Even in monster films like *Godzilla*, there's a sense of tragedy in killing the antagonist creature. Not in zombie films. These monsters are already dead, and the fact that they're walking about is a perversion of the humanity they once possessed, not a continuation of it. There's no regret in gunning down, chopping up, burning, or otherwise destroying these creatures. This allows directors and writers to create plenty of gory, tense moments using a villain that they can dispatch over and over again with no real moral consequences for the audience or the story.

The Origin Story

Zombies in film usually have some sort of origin story, of course. The various types of zombies that arise from those different stories are explored in later chapters. As an introduction, however, it's easy to see how zombie films play on current social fears to create their monsters, and to make sure that the origins are appropriately sinister.

In *Night of the Living Dead*, there's little time given to the origin of the zombies, though they apparently came back to life as the result of radiation released from an exploding space probe. In later films, the military is blamed, such as in *Return of the Living Dead*. In modern zombie films, the source of the problem is oftentimes a contagion, as seen in *28 Days Later*. Of course, mad scientists also play a part in some zombie problems, particularly in films such as *Re-Animator* and the *Resident Evil* series.

Science has rapidly displaced black magic as the culprit of zombie creation, which was the convention in films prior to *NOTLD*, with some notable exceptions.

In *White Zombie*, widely considered the first true zombie film, , Bela Lugosi plays a wicked character who uses mind control and magic to create slaves. This is in line with the traditional stories of zombies, which go back to Africa and are particularly prevalent in Haiti and other Caribbean island cultures. In those stories, the dead are brought back to life by evil Vodou priests and stories involve them being used as slave labor on sugar plantations and for other nefarious purposes. The fear in this story, of course, is that you cannot escape the brutality of life, even if you're dead.

Traditional zombie stories were given a veneer of scientific credibility by researchers who believed that specific drugs might have been used to induce a trance-like state in people. According to such thinking, Vodou priests would use a blend of drug-induced stupor and the victim's beliefs in the priest's power and the resurrection of the dead, to enslave them. Those stories sometimes involve the victim being buried alive so that they would accept the idea that they were dead psychologically and act accordingly. This is explored in the film *The Serpent and the Rainbow*, which is based on a book of the same name by anthropologist Wade Davis. These theories are not widely accepted, but they make for truly chilling tales.

In today's zombie films, everything from disease to genetic engineering is used as backstory for the zombies. Those backstories often play a significant part in how the zombies are portrayed. Zombies that are created via Vodou rituals, for example, are usually mindless, dead-eyed, and utter slaves to their creators.

In the 1960s, 1970s, and 1980s, most zombies were shambling creatures, decayed and partially decomposed.

In the 2000s, we saw the rise of the plague zombies, who are oftentimes not rotted, but who look deathly ill. Unfortunately for the living characters in those films, those plague zombies are usually fast, strong, and incredibly aggressive. Given that they don't need to breathe, zombies chasing after intended victims can make for terrifying scenes.

However they come about, zombies are great film antagonists. Whether one feels sympathy for them, or just terror and disgust, however, derives from their origins. Those zombies made by Vodou priests are really victims, even when they're frightening. The zombies that are engineered or diseased, however, are truly monsters and usually die in droves, sometimes in spectacular ways.

What to Expect

Zombie films fall squarely in the horror genre, possibly one of the most underrated genres of all time. While some of the films in this book follow pretty standard norms as far as their storytelling and action go, the fact that those norms even exist says a lot about how much people love zombie stories.

In the chapters and featured films that follow, expect something beyond conventional fear. Expect paranoia, disgust, and anxiety. Expect plenty of jump scares, but also expect menace and sustained tension. Expect characters who range from outright heroes to antiheros to villains who are only helping the likeable protagonists out of convenience.

The most important thing to keep an eye out for is diversity. Despite there being many conventions for zombie films, and despite the fact that many writers and directors stick to them rather faithfully, they also manage to create innovative films based on them. Whether it's the wit of *Zombieland*, the all-out gore of *Dead Alive,* or the visceral and memorable terror that films such as *28 Days Later* invoke, zombies work. They have endured for decades and, in fact, have become more popular than ever before. Zombies have also crossed over into so many different types of media, particularly video games, which have become even more complex.

There are plenty of ways to look at, analyze, understand, and interpret zombies and zombie films. The bottom line, however, is that zombies can serve as symbolic stand-ins for a range of social and personal fears and, given that horror films are all about fear, zombies are among the most versatile antagonists out there. Prepare to learn a lot more about zombies, to read a variety of interpretations of their meanings and, of course, to learn about some fine films—or at least thoroughly enjoyable ones—that make for hours of tarrying entertainment.

Chapter 2

What Is a Zombie?

A zombie can actually be several different things. If you're looking at the folklore zombie from Haiti and some African traditions, a zombie is a being who is either dead or who thinks they're dead and who is under the control of a Vodou practitioner. The film definition of the zombie, however, can be something quite different. To make it even more complex, film zombies have evolved over the years and are very different to those in the earliest zombie films.

The most important thing to remember about zombies, regardless of the minor variations, there are only two main types, and they add very different qualities to the films that they appear in.

To Shoot or Not to Shoot?

In the event that a zombie is controlled by a Vodou master, any evil the zombie does is really just a reflection of the evil will of the

Vodou master. Those zombies present some complexity. In *White Zombie*, for instance, the zombies live miserable existences providing slave labor to Bela Lugosi's villain, aptly named Murder, who uses his Vodou powers to keep them under control.

Because of this, there's a real moral issue with killing these zombies. The best way to handle them, in fact, is to kill the Vodou master and, by doing so, to free the zombies so that they can return to being human. Presumably, if the zombies are actuallydead once the link to the Vodou master was severed, they would cease to appear alive.

These zombies, as happens in *White Zombie*, are oftentimes surreptitiously slipped a poison by the Vodou master or someone working for him.

While they will be dealt with more extensively later in the chapter, the modern incarnations of zombies provide something much different.

To Shoot

In modern portrayals, zombies are villains that can be dispatched without any moral issues. They're either dead and resurrected, or they're infected with something that makes them too dangerous to live.

This opens up great potential, of course, for adding an element of action to horror films. This is something that video game designers have picked up on and, in some cases, films such as *Resident Evil* have managed to take what video game designers figured out and translate it to the screen.

In horror films, if there is a big bad character who is some sort of undead, they usually have a backstory and sometimes a sympathetic one. In the *Friday the 13th* franchise, for instance, Jason Voorhees was really a victim. He was a mentally challenged child who drowned as a result of the camp counselors negligence and, thus, his

Chapter 2: What Is a Zombie?

rampages are partially acts of revenge. Dracula, particularly in the 1992 version of the story, has a very sympathetic background. He's evil, but he didn't really mean to be evil.

Where zombies are concerned, particularly from *Night of the Living Dead* on, there isn't even any good or evil involved. The zombies, in essence, are just killing machines. Either they shamble across the land in a slow wave, or they sprint through the cities killing everyone in their path. There needn't be any conflicted feelings involved in gunning them down. It's kill or be killed.

That makes it possible to put some gory zombie kills into the films, of course, which has become a significant part of just about every zombie film made in the 21st century. Looking at the origins of zombies provides a good path to work our way up to the modern zombie film.

Vodou Origins

The Vodou origins of zombies are much more complex than the zombie stories of popular culture. In order to understand these stories, one has to go all the way back to Africa, where scholars believe the entire story originates.

According to the University of Michigan, the word "zombie" comes from a Kongo word, "nzambi," which means "soul." That word, over time, made its way to Haiti during the era of the slave trade, where it morphed into the word "zonbi."

According to the same source, the connection between the word "zombie" and the Kongo word for "soul" is not difficult to understand, given some of the basic beliefs in Vodou. According to Vodou beliefs, how one dies makes a big difference in how their afterlife turns out. If one dies of natural causes, they're free to join their ancestors. If one dies of unnatural causes, however, they cannot go on to meet their ancestors until the gods clear the way for them.

This places the soul in a sort of limbo, with the soul stranded at its grave and vulnerable to Vodou masters who may be able to enslave the soul.

A Vodou practitioner can capture this soul in a bottle and use it to either control the body of the deceased, or simply keep the soul.

This is what we see in the film *White Zombie*, more or less. When the villain poisons Madeline and Charles, they slowly turn into zombies and he gains complete control over them.

There are some obviously frightening aspects to this type of zombie, mainly the idea that someone could capture the soul of another human being and make that person into their servant. However, the cannibalism and other horrific aspects of zombies that are seen in modern films aren't present in these stories. What was scary then was becoming a zombie, not being eaten by one. In the film *The Serpent and the Rainbow*, the zombie is looked at in a scientific way. In this film, featured later in the book, the premise is that zombies are real, but can be explained in scientific terms.

In Ed Wood's *Plan 9 from Outer Space*, there's a combination of the Vodou mind control story and the scientific explanation. The aliens resurrect the dead, but they control them through electronic devices.

This somewhat bridges the gap between traditional zombie stories, which involve supernatural powers and souls, and modern zombie stories, which usually involve an explicable cause for the dead rising from their graves, even if the characters in the film don't know what it is. In fact, in some zombie films, the tension is amplified by a hunt for the cure.

Weird Fiction and the Zombie

Various versions of zombies—or creatures that attack like zombies in modern films—can be found in weird fiction, a genre that existed at the end of the 19th and early 20th centuries. One of weird fiction's premier writers, H.P. Lovecraft, loosely based one film, *Re-Animator*, on a weird fiction story. In that story, Herbert West is a sort of Victor Frankenstein character who attempts to raise the dead through medical means. His experiments go awry, of course, and he pays a horrible price at the hands of the creatures that he brought into the world.

One of the most common tropes in the modern zombie film is a massive zombie assault. In most cases, the protagonists have to barricade themselves into a secure location and wait out the zombies, while the creatures are battering at the doors. At some point, the zombies break through, taking lives in the process. This happens in *Night of the Living Dead, Dawn of the Dead,* and its remake, *Day of the Dead* and *28 Days Later,* among others.

An early version of this assault can be found in the William Hope Hodgson story, *The House on the Borderland*. In the story, the creatures are apparently from another dimension. They resemble swine, but are humanoid in their overall appearance. At one point in the story, the man has to hole up in his mansion with a rifle, keeping the beasts from his door. This is a scenario that closely resembles a modern zombie attack. The creatures in Hodgson's story, however, are portrayed as rather intelligent. Nonetheless, any reader who is a fan of modern zombie films will see some similarities here.

The Contaminated/Diseased Zombie

In most modern films, the zombies are created by way of contamination. This is the case in serious films, such as *Night of the Living Dead*. Here, a mysterious form of radiation makes its way back to Earth when a probe is explodes in the atmosphere. The radiation creates the zombies.

When zombies aren't created by radiation, the cause is usually biological. In *Dead Alive*, for instance, the zombies are created via an infection transmitted by the bite of the Sumatran Rat-Monkey. In *28 Days Later*, the zombies are infected with a virus that has symptoms similar to that of rabies, turning them into fast, strong, and relentless killing machines.

In some cases, the zombies are created deliberately and it's the release of either the pathogen or the zombies themselves into the wider world that creates the problem. In the *Resident Evil* franchise, for instance, the zombies are created by the T-virus and are more mutant than undead.

Because contamination spreads from person to person, a bite is oftentimes a sentence to become a zombie. The infection might itself be lethal or an infected individual may just carry the infection until they die of some other cause, at which point they become a zombie. This is one area wherein the filmmakers can set up a moral dilemma

In films, when a character's loved one becomes a zombie, the character is obligated to finish them off. This makes it especially painful for the character to deal with the loss of their loved one, given that they have to watch them die once and then kill them again. This is particularly well done in the remake of *Dawn of the Dead*, where a character's gradual transformation into a zombie is pulled off convincingly with makeup that gradually shows them taking on the characteristic appearance of a zombie.

Not all zombies fit so neatly into this description, however.

The Undead

For something to be undead, it actually has to have died and been reanimated. In folklore, there's usually something supernatural involved in "un-death." Vampires, ghouls, ghosts, and other similar creatures can all be considered undead. Through various means, they have been brought back to life, but they're not alive in the same way that a natural creature is alive.

In Romero's films, such as the *Return of the Living Dead* series and *Dead Alive*, the zombies have died. After their bodies die, they come back to life, but they're shadows of what they were before they died. In Romero's films, for instance, the dead gradually start to relearn what they knew in life, but they're not fully human. It's implied that the process of dying and being brought back has diminished them in many regards.

In other films, death doesn't really figure into the equation so much and the zombies are technically alive, but dangerously altered from their former selves.

Blending in Vampires

Two films in this book, *The Last Man on Earth* and *I Am Legend,* are based on a Richard Matheson book called *I Am Legend*. In these films, the zombies have strong elements of vampire folklore built into them.

In *The Last Man on Earth*, the easiest way to dispatch the undead is to drive a wooden stake through their hearts. They're also averse to garlic and daylight, hallmarks of vampire lore. In fact, what are essentially zombies, are called vampires in *The Last Man on Earth*. The story, however, from the way that the bacteria that causes vampirism spreads, closely resembles modern zombie films more than it does most vampire films.

I Am Legend follows a similar pattern. In that film, the dead rise after being infected with a mutation of the measles virus. It makes them strong and fast, but they're adverse to daylight. The protagonist spends his days foraging for supplies and trying to contact other survivors—along with his dog—but has to take shelter at night. In that film, the antagonists are called Darkseekers.

Most modern zombie films lack these vampiric elements, however, many of them involve creatures that are technically not undead at all, creating still another variant.

The Infected Zombie

An article in *The Vancouver Sun* looked into something that should be obvious for any fan of zombie films. In many modern films, zombies represent a fear of disease and of medical technology gone awry. When the disease spreads, it ends up destroying civilization and upsetting the natural order, playing into the fears of social collapse that have become prevalent over the years.

An infected zombie is not always undead. In the film *28 Days Later*, for instance, shooting a zombie has more in common with putting down Old Yeller than it does with driving a stake through Dracula's heart.

This trope has taken over zombie lore in recent years. Even in the television series *The Walking Dead*, a scientist character is brought in early on to provide insight into the origins of the zombie plague. They determine how it resurrects the dead and turns them into flesh-eating monsters. Audiences, it appears, are no longer willing to buy into the story of a Vodou master keeping someone's soul in a bottle, and they prefer a scientific explanation.

The infected zombie story is terrifying because it mirrors real-life plagues. From the Black Plague to the Spanish Flu to the H1N1 virus, humanity has endured illnesses that have taken thousands—sometimes millions—of lives and that have spread quickly, particularly in major urban centers. In fact, real-world doctors used a video game zombie plague to better understand how infections can spread in real life.

That incident occurred in 2005 and involved the video game *World of Warcraft*. In the game, an undead villain was introduced that infected people with "Corrupted Blood." This was what is called a "DOT"—damage over time—affliction, which slowly drained the life away from characters.

Chapter 2: What Is a Zombie?

World of Warcraft is what is called a Massively Multi-Player Role Playing Game, or MMORPG. In an MMORPG, there can be thousands of players on one server and they interact freely, as they would in real life.

There was a bug in the game that allowed characters to carry Corrupted Blood from the scenario where they were infected to densely populated areas of the game. It could spread from one character to another by proximity, much like any real-life virus.

When Corrupted Blood made it back to populated areas, they were devastated. Characters started dropping dead left and right. Lower level characters are much weaker than higher level characters, mirroring populations that are most affected in real-life plagues, such as the elderly and very young. It got weirder.

To contain the virus, the company behind the game instituted a quarantine policy that was entirely voluntary. It failed. Soon enough, people were evacuating their characters to non-populated areas. Other characters began spreading the plague deliberately, which has parallels in real life. In film, consider the original *Dawn of the Dead* from 1978. There is a conflict between law enforcement and people who refuse to bring their dead for disposal, therefore further spreading the plague.

According to reporting in Gamasutra, healer characters even started volunteering to care for characters who were infected. Even in the game world there are doctors, so to speak, who are willing to risk their own lives to save their fellows.

Researchers have expressed a great deal of interest in studying this incident, as it provides many parallels to real-life incidents of diseases spreading. Interestingly, you'll see most of these behaviors in zombie films where the dead are raised—or people are merely infected—by a virus or bacteria. Some people will try to cure it, others will flee and to avoid it and still others will, unwittingly or intentionally, spread the virus. In any case, the normal order of things is disrupted and therein lies the horror.

The beginning of a zombie plague almost always entails one particular outcome: the end of everything else.

The Bringers of the End

Some zombie films start at the beginning of the end. *Night of the Living Dead, Dawn of the Dead* (both versions) and *Resident Evil* begin as the zombies are rising up from their graves. Other films start out after the end has already come, including *Day of the Dead, 28 Weeks Later,* and *The Last Man on Earth.*

Certain things, however, have to occur to bring civilization down in these stories, and they usually occur quite reliably.

First, people are taken by surprise. *Night of the Living Dead* is a prime example of this. When it was made, it also took audiences by surprise, as they had no idea what they were about to see when they bought their tickets. In these movies, including comedies such as *Shaun of the Dead*, the characters usually don't know what's happening at first. The remake of *Dawn of the Dead* does this particularly well, with one of the protagonists trying to flee as society literally collapses in front of her.

Second, the authorities are unable to respond effectively. This is oftentimes a case of simply being overwhelmed. Each time the living dead kill someone, if they don't devour them entirely, that person presumably rises to join their ranks, creating an endless supply. In other cases, the virus may spread so quickly that the authorities cannot contain it, such as in *28 Days Later.*

With the authorities unable to respond effectively, civil order collapses. This results in all cohesion breaking down and, most of the time, in humanity splitting up into small bands. In *Dawn of the Dead*, we see this as the protagonists realize their best chance of survival is to steal a helicopter and to get as far away from the city as possible. The zombie apocalypse has become so ingrained into society, in fact, that there are many Web pages and books dedicated to showing

Chapter 2: What Is a Zombie?

people how to build a zombie survival kit. The CDC even picked up on this, issuing zombie survival instructions that serve equally as well as instructions on how to survive any natural disaster. The CDC doesn't currently recommend obtaining a shotgun or a machete, however, though this is the case for the sites and books that take the matter less seriously.

Why would an fictional scenario work for emergencies as well as actual survival instructions? Again, because this scenario plays on real-life fears. While they may be on much smaller scales, riots, terrorist attacks, disease outbreaks, natural disasters, and other catastrophes can closely parallel the nature of fictional zombie attacks. People need to have food, water, transportation, an escape plan, means of communication, medication, and tools to help them survive.

Horror films take genuinely scary scenarios and allow the audience to experience them without putting themselves in harm's way. In the case of zombie films, particularly those that play into modern fears, we get to watch society collapse without having to lose any of what it has to offer. When we go home after the movie, the lights still turn on, the water still runs, and our neighbors aren't trying to steal our supplies or eat us. For the runtime of the film, however, we get to enjoy a sort of roller coaster ride that takes us through some of our most significant and widely shared anxieties.

The Survival Fantasy

Part of the fantasy of zombie films is the idea of survival. In these films, the group of survivors tends to have enough weapons, food, and other supplies to endure for a long time. In reality, the weight of the water one human being needs to survive for even a week is a great deal to carry.

In some cases, the filmmakers avoid getting too farfetched by having the main characters join up with people who would be equipped for hardship, such as military units or survivalists. In some cases, even someone with hunting and camping skills—Darryl from *The Walking Dead* is a great example—becomes incredibly valuable to the survivors, as they could not get by without their assistance.

If one were to look at it objectively, the only chance that most people would have of surviving the zombie apocalypse would be to stick together as much as possible.

One film that happens to pull off the hardships of the zombie apocalypse is *Night of the Living Dead*. In that film, none of the characters have any convenient skills that improve their chances. None of the characters happens to have an arsenal of weapons handy or a means of communication. The characters, for the most part, don't even get along, and some of them—Barbara and Harry—are dead weight or outright liabilities.

In real life, what happened in *World of Warcraft* seems to be far more likely to occur. Those that can, try to heal the sick. People tend to warn one another of the risk of becoming infected and, even though these people try to keep it together, there are those who will spread the disease and, inevitably, the disease will take out a large chunk of the population.

In short, if you're planning to survive the zombie apocalypse, the most realistic way to do it is to just give in and become a zombie. If you're planning on holing up with a group of survivors, you're likely to find that things fall apart fast and that sooner or later, everyone becomes infected.

In the next chapter, we'll look at how zombies have been portrayed in film over the years. Building on what's already been established, you'll find that the fears of the time often have a strong influence on the design of the monsters.

http://www.vancouversun.com/entertainment/movie-guide/psychology+scary+Zombies+deepest+fears+death/9089665/story.html

http://www.umich.edu/~uncanny/zombies.html

http://www.cdc.gov/phpr/zombies.htm

http://www.gamasutra.com/php-bin/news_index.php?story=18571

Chapter 3

Zombie Physiology: The Anatomy of the Dead

Chapter 4 deals with how zombies have been portrayed in films throughout the years, but it's useful to look at the creatures themselves first. Zombies have evolved a great deal since *White Zombie* chilled audiences with its tale of necromancy, mind control, and ancient folk legends. Today's zombies are typically far less mystical than they were in the past, but far deadlier as well. Let's look at how filmmakers have made zombies into more than the sum of their parts or, in some cases, made them precisely the sum of their parts.

Wave After Wave

Zombies may have spilled a lot of blood over the years, but just as much ink has been spilled writing about them. It's easier to understand what zombies actually are if you make a simple distinction.

The Controlled, Reanimated Dead

This type of zombie includes the traditional zonbi, as described in Haitian folklore, as well as more modern zombies that predate film portrayals starting in the 1950s and 1960s.

These zombies are usually few in number, and are controlled by some sort of a master—be that a scientist or a Vodou practitioner—and have been raised from the grave intentionally. Examples include anything from the zombies in *White Zombies* to the reanimated corpse in *Frankenstein*.

These zombies are usually characterized as slow-moving, behaving as if they're sleepwalking or drugged, but not always. This is precisely the story used in *The Serpent and the Rainbow*: a drug is used to put people in a sort of suspended animation, then Vodou practitioners reanimate people after they appear to die, and those people become the walking dead.

These types of zombies tend to mix the supernatural with science in terms of their explanations.

The Serpent and the Rainbow also provides a fine example of science and superstition crossing paths. The researcher in the film, Alan, is looking for a drug that can provide a more effective form of anesthetic. He does manage to discover a scientific explanation for much of what happens in Haiti, but certainly some of it defies explanation, as well.

This type of zombie is not as popular as it used to be and has largely been supplanted by zombies that have more to do with Romero than they do with Haiti. The science and supernatural crossover is often still there, but the results are much different and the danger is oftentimes increased.

It's key to remember that, in a story that involves a Vodou-style zombie, the real danger is usually the person who makes and controls those zombies. The threat is that the protagonist might become zombies themselves. Today's zombies are far different things.

The Horde

Most modern zombies in film can be traced back to George Romero's *Night of the Living Dead* in terms of their behaviors, their physiology, and their origins. They tend to have certain things in common.

First, zombies are generally mindless, though Romero's zombies seem to evolve as the movies go on. In the *Return of the Living Dead* series, the zombies are shown to have at least some intelligence, the ability to talk, and the ability to understand that certain actions yielded certain results: i.e., eating brains kills the pain of being dead.

In most films, however, the zombies are, for the most part, a mindless horde that eat anything in their path. There's some variation in terms of "anything in their path", however. Zombies always kill and, most often, consume human beings. They may or may not eat other animals. In the remake of *Dawn of the Dead*, for instance, a dog manages to move its way through a crowd of hungry zombies, not garnering any interest from them until it's about to run through a door. It's not clear whether the zombie that goes for the dog wants to eat it or if it just figured out that the dog will lead it to another living human being.

Second, the zombies don't eat one another. They eat the living but, in a horde of zombies, it's not common to see them turn on one another. In Romero's films, the evolving zombies even start to show signs of compassion for one another, even if they view living human beings as lunch.

Third, these zombies may attack in small groups or en mass This is largely a matter of plot convenience. The nature of these attacks also tends to follow the law of the Conservation of Ninjitsu as detailed by TV Tropes. This means that whether there is one zombie or thirty zombies, they tend to present an equal threat. If one zombie corners a hero character, it'll be a very tough fight to kill it off, often involving a struggle where the hero finally finds something that allows them to take out the zombie. If there are thirty zombies, the hero will either cut them down as if they were wheat waiting to be reaped, or will just avoid them. A sufficiently sized horde almost always results in the main characters having to flee or barricade themselves into a space where they can put up some sort of a defense.

Fourth, modern zombies usually spread the zombie plague themselves, not requiring there to be a Vodou practitioner, mad scientist, or alien mastermind to do it. It's oftentimes spread through a bite, making zombification very similar to rabies in many regards. Provided there is enough left of someone who is killed in a zombie attack, their corpse will reanimate and become a zombie itself, continuing the plague.

That fourth element is vital, because it's the element that allows zombies to be presented as threats to not only the main characters, but to society overall. Modern zombies are merely vessels for whatever plague is caused the outbreak, providing a way for the problem to spread. They're not serving anyone's conscious desires and, in fact, are basically nightmare versions of a sneeze that spreads a bad cold through an office.

These types of zombies are, by far, more common in modern films. There are even films that imply some level of zombie domestication, such as *Fido, Day of the Dead,* and so forth. These films, however, usually have an underlying threat presented by the fact that the zombie, even if it's learning, still sees human beings as food and can turn them into zombies.

Making Sense of It All

Understanding the physiology of a Vodou zombie is not difficult. They're basically human beings. Particularly if they're drugged, no supernatural or odd scientific explanation is required. They're simply under the influence of a toxin, and because their culture has predisposed them to believing that a Vodou master could control them, they act as they feel they should act: like a reanimated corpse. What's going on in these cases is a sort of stage hypnosis where the victim has to believe that the Vodou has power for it to work. If they don't believe it, presumably the drug's effects would end. In essence, if the victim believed in the power of drugs more than they did the power of Vodou, they might see the Vodou master as someone who drugged them, rather than as someone who took control of their soul.

Modern zombies are where things get complex. Let's look at some examples and how they work.

The Physiology of the Actual Reanimated Dead

Suspension of disbelief occurs when one takes in information that conflicts with what they generally know to be true, and chooses to believe it anyway. Without suspension of disbelief, zombie films wouldn't work.

Zombies are usually portrayed as having only one weak point: their brain. You have to score a headshot to take them out. Chop off their arm and you have a one-armed zombie chasing you. Chop off their leg and you have a zombie limping after you. Nothing but a shot to the brain will kill them.

In reality, this just doesn't make sense, given how the human body itself works. No matter how they try to explain it away in the script, the human body cannot function if only the brain is working. Unless the zombies are infected but still living, there's always an element of the supernatural in a living dead film.

The Rotting Problem

Right now, our bodies are fighting a battle they will fight until the day we die, at which point it will lose. Our bodies are constantly under attack, particularly by bacteria and insects—we have tiny insects all over our bodies, disturbing as that may be to consider—that are slowly eating us alive. When we die, we no longer replenish skin cells so eventually they consume our bodies and, as the expression states, turning us back into dust.

The way that zombies move in films implies some sort of rigor mortis. The stiff, jerky movements also indicate that their bodies are decaying to some degree. Oftentimes, the scariest zombies in films are those that are in the most advanced state of decay, with exposed bone and muscle tissue. Their clothing may also be rotted, implying a long wait in the ground before the radiation, virus, or whatever else is caused them to rise.

The site Cracked did a great breakdown of how rot would actually affect zombies. Inside us, right now, there are huge populations of bacteria. Some of this bacterium is actually helpful, facilitating digestion. However, when we die, that bacteria starts to grow out of control, eventually consuming our entire bodies, or at least what parts of it that maggots, cockroaches, birds and other scavengers don't get to first.

In short, while those zombie hordes are trying to eat the living, there are far more creatures trying to eat those zombies.

Rotting is inevitable. The zombie hordes depicted banging on the boarded-up doors and windows, in reality, would start falling apart very quickly. If you want a (rather disturbing) example of this, leave some old meat outside on a hot summer day. It won't take long to attract, wasps, and other creatures that will begin to eat and lay eggs in it. Within a couple of days, you should have a pretty good collection of ants and maggots munching away at the meat and, before too long, that meat will be stripped to the bone. That's exactly what would happen to undead zombies. Surviving a zombie apocalypse would involve a lot more waiting than shooting and machete swinging.

One of the ways that writers get around this is by having the plague spread so quickly that every time one zombie drops, another rises to take its place. Even this wouldn't last for too long. Without new hosts to infect, the plague would inevitably fizzle out.

Fast and Infected: Zombie Variants

Two modern films provide very good examples of how zombies have evolved in movies. The world of zombie films changed with the introduction of the fast zombie and living-but-infected zombie. Oftentimes, they are one and the same.

The Need for Speed

New films that cover the same ground as previous films tend to become tedious very quickly. There's only so much time a group of survivors can spend hiding out in a house while zombies pound at the door before the concept becomes boring.

Enter the fast zombie.

In the 2004 remake of *Dawn of the Dead*, the first zombie we see is a fast zombie. The little girl who bites Ana's husband moves frighteningly fast, in fact. Because audiences were so accustomed to slow, shambling zombies, this portrayal was particularly effective. It wasn't the first time zombies had been shown moving quickly, but there's a difference between this film and *28 Days Later,* which is explored in the next section, that makes *Dawn of the Dead* notable for its use of this type of zombie.

These zombies are basically variations on the Romero zombie, with the ability to move at speeds comparable to, or in excess of, what a typical human being can reach. Here's the catch: they don't get tired. While the prospect of trying to outrun a slow horde of zombies is scary, the fast zombie is even scarier.

To outrun the shamblers, one only need maintain a lead that allows them to rest before the horde catches up. The main threat is being surrounded or cornered, at which point all hope is lost.

Outrunning fast zombies, unless you can get to shelter or a weapon, is essentially impossible. As portrayed in most movies since *Dawn of the Dead*, these zombies move at around the speed of a very fast sprinter, except they're not going to run out of breath, given that they're not breathing.

Unlike the hordes that stupidly pound at doors, fast zombies tend to attack structures with some enthusiasm as well. They'll tear at doors and try to crawl through car windows. They're every bit as frightening as having a living, homicidal person after you.

Zombie films might be about having a good time more than anything else, but that doesn't mean that fast zombies aren't controversial. The concept was a major change for the genre, and one that required the protagonists to react to threats in an entirely different way.

Escaping the Fast Zombies

When zombies are slow and the protagonists make a break for it, they can usually engage in a sort of running battle. They can use firearms to take out the zombies that are close to them without having to worry about those further away. As long as you see them coming, there's plenty of time to close the door before they get in. Even if you're surprised and only one zombie that made it to the door, it's easy enough to push them back. This is not the case with the fast zombies.

The fast zombies require the characters to have a very different strategy for survival, and to act more quickly when they're threatened. The final chase sequence in *Dawn of the Dead*, when the characters run to the harbor to get the boat, requires them to fortify a bus and to move very quickly. When they run into trouble, there isn't a lot of time for them to plan their next move.

In *28 Days Later*, once the zombies spot humans or get close, they don't have much time and they need to move fast. This increases the tension in these films considerably. It also allows the director to use fewer zombies to represent a real threat. One of these fast zombies chasing humans up a flight of stairs, for example, is a more significant threat than ten or twenty slow zombies doing the same.

Of course, it's also a lot harder to score a headshot on a zombie who's moving at a full sprint than it is on one who's is slowly lurching its way over. With the fast zombies, the characters pretty much have one shot or they're dead, which is great for making zombie films more intense.

The Plague Zombies

Resident Evil and *28 Days Later*, and *I Am Legend*, are all among the films that have given us zombies created by a scientifically explainable plague. These zombies are usually quite different from the walking dead type in that, technically, they're still alive.

In *Resident Evil*, the zombies are dead but going through a process of mutation into other creatures. In *I Am Legend*, a plague has infected the world and the zombies are infected individuals who have mutated. *28 Days Later*, however, depicts perhaps the most chilling incarnation of the plague zombie.

In *28 Days Later*, the zombies are created when human beings are infected with the Rage virus. That virus is built on the popular concept of rabies, more or less, but it's much worse.

Humans infected with rabies suffer symptoms that affect the brain. Rabies might seem like a disease from a different era, but even with modern medicine, it's still quite terrifying. In fact, according to the CDC, only ten people are known to have survived this infection, and only two of those didn't receive the recommended treatment.

Rabies starts out the way most zombie infections start out in these films. The person gets flu-like symptoms, including a high fever and a headache. This goes on for some time. The worst symptoms appear much later. The person starts hallucinating, quite often, and becomes agitated. Most of the time, within ten days, the person who contracted rabies will be dead.

When people think of rabies—and the origin of the word is "rabid", in fact—they think of the kind of aggressive response to the infection that one sees in animals. Rabid animals will sometimes attack without provocation and without any signs of fear. Unfortunately, the virus is transmitted via bites, so there's some evolutionary advantage to this method of spreading for the virus itself.

This is very close to how the zombie virus spreads in films. In *28 Days Later*, the infected behave much as one would expect a rabid dog or other animal to behave. They're agitated and homicidal. The way that they attack, of course, spreads Rage even further.

This sort of a scenario obviously has roots in real-life plagues. Plagues can hit without warning and spread incredibly fast, particularly when people move around as much as they do in modern times.

SARS, Severe Acute Respiratory Syndrome, was a prime example of this. In 2003, the virus managed to spread incredibly fast because of international travel. In *28 Days Later,* the lead character has been in a coma for 28 days. When he wakes up, he finds that during those weeks, the Rage virus has completely devastated the UK. The entire UK, in fact, has been quarantined.

Chapter 3: Zombie Physiology: Anatomy of the Dead ■ 33

Here's the real nightmare: the virus spreads so fast that, in the end, the lucky ones are the ones that go first. The survivors cannot leave, as they may be infected..

The plague zombies aren't dead. They're infected. This means that, somewhere underneath all the delirium and other effects of the virus, they still have somewhere near a human level of intelligence. If they hear you, they'll investigate. If they see lights on, they'll investigate. Fast zombies aren't only fast from a physical perspective, but also from a mental perspective, making them even more dangerous.

Like the rabid animals that they're partially modeled after, these zombies are hyper-aggressive. They attack without hesitation and without fear. Presumably driven mad by their infections, they seek to kill anyone and anything they come across.

Are fast zombies a betrayal of the zombie as a monster? Some might think so, but zombies have evolved significantly over the years. They've gone from mind-controlled slaves to the risen undead, to shambling hordes, to creatures that can understand how to use tools and that hold grudges and have friends. Today's films, without a doubt, tend to be darker than the films of the past, particularly where horror is concerned. Fast zombies are, to some degree, an example of that.

Sometimes it's useful to think about this in terms of what the characters have available to them. In *Night of the Living Dead*, Ben had a hunting rifle and not much more. In films set in modern times, particularly in the US, it's not unrealistic to have characters equipped with fast-firing semi-automatic firearms and some degree of fighting ability. Additionally, female characters have evolved from ones who fall after losing a shoe, only to scream until they are killed, to characters who are just as capable—and sometimes more so—than the males. Fast weapons, developed skills, and more teamwork mean that a higher caliber of antagonist is required and that's just what fast zombies offer.

Add this to the fact that we live in a world governed far more by science than by superstition, and plague zombies make a lot more sense than undead zombies rising from their graves. However far-fetched it might be, the scientific explanation requires less suspension of disbelief and, while the undead are fictional creatures, infected, mad and dangerous people are not.

The Mutant or Engineered Zombie

This modern zombie variant is created specifically for some purpose, usually military or scientific. There is some similarity here with the zombies in *28 Days Later,* but in that case, it was the virus that was engineered.

Resident Evil and the *Return of the Living Dead* franchises both provide good examples of engineered zombies. In the former film, the zombies are just one result of the T-virus, which escapes The Hive and ends up unleashing the zombie apocalypse on civilization. In *Return of the Living Dead*, there was a zombie incident involving military chemical engineering in the past, but the entire thing was covered up. The military didn't engineer the zombies, but it did contain them and made an effort to keep them contained. This lasted until a knuckleheaded night manager at a medical supply warehouse and his equally knuckleheaded trainee set them loose once more.

Mutant zombies often have powers and a physiology that far removes them from a standard zombie. They may, for example, be like the Licker creature in *Resident Evil,* which is basically a dog that's mutated to the point where it's unrecognizable. In that film, we see the Umbrella Corporation, at the end, taking away a man who has started to mutate for a project named "Nemesis." There's a strong implication that, at the same time as they're trying to contain the damage, the corporation in this film is also trying to direct the damage in a way that suits their profits.

In *I Am Legend*, genetic engineering leads to the end of civilization as well. In this case, however, it's good intentions that pave the road to hell. In that film, a would-be cure for cancer is what leads to the zombie apocalypse. Whether their intentions were good, bad, or greedy, people unwittingly engineer the zombie apocalypse quite often in these films. Even in *Night of the Living Dead*, it was science that lead to the dead rising from their graves, albeit not intentionally. The difference, however, comes in whether or not the scientists actually engineered the zombies themselves or just engineered the cause of the disease.

Chapter 4

Zombie Physiology Part II: Killing a Zombie

If you're lucky, you'll be a genetically engineered killer like Alice from *Resident Evil*, and the zombie apocalypse will be a world in which you're well suited for survival. Since you're probably not, you'll want to look at how the protagonists kill off the zombies in these films. There are many commonalities between the various films, and some of them are canon between one film and the next.

Remember the Different Types

Zombie films usually provide a morality-free killing spree for the survivors. Everyone they're killing is either already dead, or inevitably headed that way due to some sort of infection. They all present a threat, so the survivors can kill them without ever wondering if they're doing the right thing.

In the case of a Vodou zombie, remember that they're actually human beings under the control of a Vodou master. In *White Zombie*, for instance, the zombies that die at the end of the film were presumably human beings who would have reverted once Murder was killed. This introduces a moral dimension in that the zombies in these stories are really victims, not maniacs.

It also means that, in those cases, one can kill zombies using any method that would kill a regular human being. They're not dead, so a stab wound to the chest would be just as deadly to them as it would be to anyone else.

When the zombies are dead—or infected—however, the way one deals with them becomes much more complicated.

Headshot

In the context of a zombie film, a 'headshot' can refer to shooting a zombie in the head with a firearm, or using a melee weapon to deliver a blow to the brain. It's the only sure way to kill off a zombie, implying that there's some sort of brain function that needs to be eliminated to take the zombie out for good. This is a great way to show that one of the protagonists is a true badass by having that character score headshot after headshot. Unfortunately, it's harder than it looks.

If you want to try this out for yourself—safely—you can do it without a gun. All you need is a laser pointer and some room to exert yourself. For the most realistic example, do this outside.

Take the laser pointer and run around for a few minutes, enough to work up a good sweat. Choose something about the size of a human head and try to hold the laser pointer steady on it. You likely will have a very hard time doing so. Now, try to do it while you're moving. It's almost impossible, even for trained individuals such as soldiers and police officers.

This means that the weapons that the characters select, and their skills before the zombie apocalypse broke out, are vital.

Chapter 4: Zombie Physiology II: Killing a Zombie

In the 1978 *Dawn of the Dead*, there's an interlude wherein a group of rednecks are shown cheerfully blasting zombies with their deer rifles. It makes sense that they'd have some skill in this, in that they were all clearly hunters before the outbreak.

You'll see this same trope played out in other venues. In the television series *The Walking Dead*, Darryl grew up in the backwoods of Georgia, hunting much of his own food. This makes him a deadly shot, an expert tracker, and a skilled hunter. This, in turn, makes him one of the best friends one can have during the zombie apocalypse.

Soldiers and police officers are also ideal companions due to their training. In the 2004 version of *Dawn of the Dead*, Kenneth and CJ are both excellent fighters with advanced firearms skills.

What does one do when they don't have those skills? Get up close and personal, unfortunately. Below is some information on the various weapons used in these films and their overall effectiveness. The thing to remember, however, is that taking out the head is the best way to take down a zombie and, sometimes, the only way.

Decapitation

Decapitation is one way to off the dead, but it's not always something that actually kills them. In *Land of the Dead*, for instance, a zombie's decapitated occurs early on in the film. Its head continues to live, however, prompting another zombie to kill it out of compassion. This is played up in *Day of the Dead* as well.

In *Return of the Living Dead*, we see a zombie get split completely in two. She continues living and, even more than that, she continues to give information to the protagonists.

In *Re-Animator*, one of the antagonist characters not only gets beheaded, but continues to control his body, despite his unfortunate predicament. If anything, it makes him even more dangerous.

Where zombies are concerned, beheading is just one more form of dismemberment and that's not fatal to them. What's fatal is destroying their head, and that's the only thing that will really do it.

Kill It With Fire!

Kill it with fire is an Internet trope and a zombie fiction trope, as well as something that pops up across many other film genres. The advantage of killing something with fire is that it results in complete incineration, which means that there's no need to watch your back when you're walking away from the kill.

One of the best examples of this can be found in the remake of *Dawn of the Dead*. The characters build improvised incendiary bombs and let them loose on the zombies, causing devastating damage.

Another advantage of fire is that one sets it and forgets about it. There's no need to set the fire more than once, as opposed to shooting several zombies individually, or swinging weapons at them while trying to get away. If they're slow, stupid zombies, they might just walk directly into the fire. Even if they don't walk into it, they would probably attempt to get away from it, allowing the protagonists to escape.

Zombie Killers and Signature Weapons

The zombie apocalypse scenario has made fantasy weapons fun again, separating them from the realm of high-fantasy sword-and-sorcery stories. Today's zombie-killing weapons don't have to be pulled out of a stone, either. You can buy them online, and they're even handy to have around for more realistic scenarios, such as camping or breaking down a door in an emergency. Let's take a look at some and the characters that make use of them.

Bows and Arrows/Crossbows

These are staples of both zombie films and video games. Of the two, crossbows are generally more effective, as there's less of a learning curve involved in shooting one accurately than there is with a standard bow.

These show up in all kinds of places, including films such as *Diary of the Dead*, and television shows such as *The Walking Dead*, where a crossbow is one of the major character's signature weapons.

The advantages of these weapons are obvious. They're quiet, which allows one to dispatch a zombie without alerting other zombies nearby. The ammunition can be recovered and used again, provided the bolt or arrow doesn't bend significantly when it hits the target.

The disadvantages of these weapons are that they're slower and bulkier than firearms, and they have fewer options in terms of shooting positions. This is somewhat mollified by crossbows, which allow the shooter to fire from a prone position.

If a bow is sturdy enough, it can be used as a bludgeoning weapon.

Despite what's shown in film, making a fast reflex shot with a bow—particularly at a target as small as a zombie's head—is very difficult, even at close range. Miss, and you'd better have something to back up that bow, because reloading really isn't an option unless you have plenty of time.

Axes and Tomahawks

Axes in this case constitute large axes, such as the emergency axe that Dan uses to defend Megan at the end of *Re-Animator*. The advantage with these types of axes is that they're widely available, incredibly durable, and easy enough to use. They're also great for practical uses. The disadvantage is that they're hard to swing and take a lot of energy to use.

This is where the tomahawk comes in. Most associated with the American frontier, this is a battle and utility axe consisting of a small head, usually with some sort of back spike and a hammer feature. Axes have long been favored as melee weapons.. They take far less skill to use than a sword, and are very durable and easy to care for. Like any axe, they're also practical. Remember that, if you're on the run from zombies, saving weight and space is imperative, so you'll want to be sure that anything you carry has more than one use.

Machetes

These show up in so many films that it's impossible to list them all. Machetes are large knives. They're usually used to cut brush in jungle environments, though there are specialized designs for the same uses in other climates. They're also used extensively in agriculture, particularly sugar cane harvesting. They're called cutlasses in many Caribbean nations, where they have strong cultural significance in addition to practical value.

Machetes and machete-like blades come in many different variations. In the *Resident Evil* series, Alice carries dual kukri knives at one point. These are a type of working/fighting blade that originates in Nepal and that is believed to be descended from swords. Many characters carry Latin American machetes, which usually have a longer and more flexible blade and are roughly the length of a short sword.

Machetes are fast, lethal and easily capable of beheading a human being. They have been used as instruments of war, and are included in some types of martial arts training, such as Filipino Eskrima. Like a tomahawk, they have practical value, are light enough to carry comfortably, and are lethal weapons.

Chapter 5

Story Structure

Many of the films featured in this book see everyday people put into situations that they're not equipped to handle. Sometimes these people end up surprising themselves and doing well in their dangerous new world. Sometimes the zombies surprise them first. In other films, there are characters who have skills that make it more likely that they'll survive and, in still other films, the characters are clearly suited for an environment where they are constantly under threat by the undead.

The zombie film is a very specific type of film, one that thrives on choosing from a number of conventions, such as those listed above, and turning them into new and interesting stories. The best films manage to do this well, taking a convention such as a group of survivors trying to make it out of an infected area, and telling that story in a completely new way.

In this chapter, we'll look at what makes zombie films work in terms of story structure. There are definitely some conventions here, but as good zombie films demonstrate, it's possible to write a story that is conventional or even predictable, and still have it be very enjoyable.

Surviving the End

Surviving the end is one of the most common motivations for characters in zombie films, and one of the go-to motivations for the action for any zombie storywriter. This story usually presumes that the characters are not in a position to stop what's going on, and that they need to stay alive at least long enough for the zombie apocalypse to pass.

A variation on this occurs when the story starts after the zombie apocalypse has already taken place, and civilization is more or less gone. Sometimes civilization is completely gone. Whatever the variation, the point of one of these stories is to survive as long as possible, and for the audience to explore how this affects the characters in the story.

Survivor Drama

Survivor drama plays a primary role in stories of this type. It can go many different ways. Here are a few to watch out for.

Factions: In many stories that involve characters just trying to survive, the group will split off into factions that end up opposing one another. In these cases, this will present an internal threat to the characters at the same time that they are being menaced by hordes of hungry undead.

Day of the Dead, the remake of *Dawn of the Dead*, *Doom*, *Resident Evil*, and even *Zombieland* have elements of this in their plot. In *Day of the Dead*, the tension is exceptionally high and turns deadly. In *Zombieland*, a zom-com, the characters scheming against one another generate the tension. In *Land of the Dead*, the faction conflict is directly related to economic class conflict, but is greatly exaggerated and far more obvious than is usually the case.

Chapter 5: Story Structure

Leader Fight: While everything is falling apart or after it has already fallen apart, characters need to decide whether they're willing to take the lead, or whether they want to help a capable leader do the same. Rest assured, there will be plenty of people jockeying for this work, and they'll sometimes get involved in a vicious fight to settle the matter.

Harry and Ben in *Night of the Living Dead* are a great example of this. Ben is the one any sensible person would follow. He's solid, intelligent, and determined. He looks for solutions and figures out ways to exploit them when he does. Harry, on the other hand, is angry, paranoid, and cowardly. He might get to be in charge, but mainly because of his emotional bullying. Leader fights pop up in the remake of *Dawn of the Dead*, too, as well as many other zombie films, and can make for great sources of tension.

Gang Fights: Once a leader with a crew established, one of the most natural things to do is to pit them against another leader and their crew. Sometimes groups of people welcome one another, and sometimes they do just the opposite.

In the remake of *Dawn of the Dead*, the mall security guards want to keep the main group of survivors out and, though they eventually do so, they are not keen on letting them in.

In *28 Days Later*, the military has run amok and the main characters end up in direct conflict with them. A similar situation happens in *Diary of the Dead*, when soldiers are shown exploiting people they come across, robbing them of most of their goods.

This type of conflict can get very involved. It dominated more than an entire season of the *Walking Dead* television franchise, for example.

The Liability: Sometimes, a character will end up holding the other survivors back, and this will be the cause of drama. It might be someone who cannot keep up with the rest of the survivors, such as the kids in *28 Weeks Later*, or pregnant Francine in *Dawn of the*

Dead. This can be a great way to set up conflict. The main conflict, of course, is always whether the characters to help the person, or are better off just letting them fall behind.

The Enemy Within: There are two versions of this and one of them doesn't work well in many newer zombie films.

The first variation occurs when one of the characters is bitten by a zombie and realizes that they're going to turn, or the group does. This can happen very slowly in older films. Both *Night of the Living Dead* and *Dawn of the Dead* use this trope to drive tension for quite a bit of the runtime. Because it takes time for the person to die and come back, the tension can be maintained in films where the zombie plague doesn't hit instantaneously. If it is a fast-acting virus, however, this is played in a different way.

In films where the cause of zombification spreads very quickly, the spread of the virus itself causes the tension. Great examples of this are the spread of Rage in the safe room in *28 Weeks Later,* and the spread of the zombie virus in the commercial airliner in *World War Z.* The spread is shown to take only minutes in both cases, with each infected person spreading the plague as soon as they're finished turning.

The drama that survivors go through is not the only drama that goes on in these films. Some of the drama is based around bigger questions and ideas and sometimes ideologies. Political and social commentary is oftentimes a significant and meaningful part of a good zombie story, and some directors are quite talented at getting their views into these films.

Political Drama, and Zombies

George Romero is particularly well known for the social commentary that's threaded throughout his scripts. Sometimes it's very subtle, such as in *Night of the Living Dead,* and sometimes it's obvious, such as in *Land of the Dead*. Other directors have managed

Chapter 5: Story Structure 47

to wedge various political messages or analogies into their works as well. Some overarching political themes are seen in many zombie films, though they may be addressed in vastly different ways between one film and the next.

Military Themes

If a zombie apocalypse ever really happened, there's no realistic way that the military would not be one of the first large institutions to respond. Whether they play a significant or insignificant role, the military will almost always be involved in a zombie film at some level. Directors can treat the military in ways that either line up with or foil other political elements in the story.

The Military Industrial Complex: This is military behaving in a way best described as Lawful Evil. In films such as *28 Weeks Later*, *Day of the Dead*, *28 Days Later*, *Return of the Living Dead*, and *Doom*, the military is portrayed as promoting some type of structure. It is also portrayed as promoting a structure you'd do well to avoid.

In *28 Days Later* and *Day of the Dead*, we see a military that's maintained its chain of command but has lost any sense of human rights or even basic civil law. The military personnel in these films become merciless, oppressive, and bullying. They seek to control or exploit anyone who isn't a part of their organization.

Often, these militaries are paired with scientific operations that are just as evil and that need a structure to survive. In *28 Weeks Later*, the military is completely cleared to fire at civilians, and they have a research facility where they seek to develop a vaccine for the virus, but where their lax security causes a disaster. In *Day of the Dead*, the military was initially in charge of protecting and assisting a group of scientists so that they could work on the vaccine and, though their alliance with the civilians was failing during the film, they started out still in that role.

In zombie films, there are few instances where combining the military and scientific expertise turns out to be a good thing. In fact, the entire problem in *28 Days Later* starts with research that has obvious military value. There are exceptions, however.

In *World War Z*, the military industrial complex is unambiguously the good-guy force in the story. They're shown doing their best to wipe out the zombies and they send a very skilled team to do it, proving that it's not a token effort. This is a rare instance in these films, where the military and scientists work to restore civilization, making it more Lawful Good than anything else.

In many zombie films, when the military teams up with science and industry, the results are disastrous. The Umbrella Corporation from the *Resident Evil* franchise, for instance, was certainly not one that would be above developing biological weapons, or building them out of existing life forms. In *Return of the Living Dead*, the military is implied to not only be responsible for creating zombies, but for hiding it from the public. In the end, they drop nukes to cover it up once and for all.

The Serpent and the Rainbow is a variation on this, taken from real life and portrayed to chilling effect.

The Tonton Macoute were a violent paramilitary force in Haiti for much of the 20th century. They were also associated with Vodou, which made them even more frightening to the population that they oppressed, and which figures prominently into the plot of *The Serpent and the Rainbow*. In that film, it's not the military industrial complex that drives much of the terror but, rather, the military religious complex, which has many sinister motives and players.

Deadly and Undisciplined: One of Romero's favorite themes, but one that isn't as common as the one described above, involves having military units that stick together, but completely abandon their chain of command. Sometimes, they may keep something of their original chain of command, simply because they're accustomed to one particular person being in charge. Staff Sergeant Crockett in

Chapter 5: Story Structure ■ 49

Survival of the Dead, for instance, is still the man, but his people have already abandoned their posts and have taken to robbing people when needed.

This is quite different from what we see in *28 Days Later*. The soldiers in that story are still very much under the command of Major West and they seem to believe that they are serving their country. They have a sense of being in the Army.

While they weren't soldiers, the security team in the remake of *Dawn of the Dead* were similar to the military group in *Diary of the Dead*. They still stuck together and didn't mind lording their power over others at the end of a gun. In the end, though, they weren't really the bad guys. That is, if their characters were redeemable. The soldiers in *Day of the Dead* were heading in this direction toward the end of the film.

Consumerism

Most people who have even a fleeting familiarity with zombie films will likely know that some are associated with critiques of consumerism. Criticism or satire of consumerism does exist in some zombie films, but it's mostly associated with the 1978 *Dawn of the Dead*. At least, that's probably what people are thinking of when they think of the connections between the two.

Some writers regard the critique of consumerism in *Dawn of the Dead* to be an excellent satire that allows very sophisticated debates over consumerism. If you're not interested in taking any of it so deeply, and there's really no obligation to do so.

One of the things that make *Dawn of the Dead* a great film is that the social commentary doesn't come at the expense of making a good movie. As What Culture pointed out in a tribute to the film, the shopping mall provides a good place to launch a critique of consumer culture, but it's also just a great location all round. It's used effectively for both commentary and by the film's characters in the movie to survive, and to keep their spirits up.

In the 2004 remake of *Dawn of the Dead*, the critique isn't quite as much a part of the film. The zombies in that film are also completely different in terms of how they move, so having them shamble slowly around a mall wouldn't have been effective.

Other films have their messages, but the commentary on consumerism in *Dawn of the Dead* is one of the most famous examples.

Scientists Gone Mad

Scientists often go mad all on their own, without being part of any larger corporate or government conspiracy. The film *The Dead Hate the Living!* for instance, has a mad scientist character that combines his scientific wizardry with black magic. In *Re-Animator*, Herbert West epitomizes the mad scientist character.

There are examples, too, of scientists who go mad for all the right reasons. In *I Am Legend*, Neville, a virologist, works feverishly to cure the plague that's turned humans into monstrosities. He repeats the same words he told his wife, that he would stay and that he could fix the plague, nearly robotically to the first person he sees in more than two years.
Morgan in *The Last Man on Earth*, derived from the same source material as *I Am Legend*, is also a scientist driven mad by trying to cure the zombie plague, but who is essentially still good.

The virologist in *World War Z* has some shades of madness to his character. He almost sounds aroused by how elegantly nature kills. Nonetheless, there's no reason to believe he ever has any intentions other than trying to stop the plague from spreading.

Underestimating nature, delving too far into secrets that are best left undiscovered, and other common tropes involving the shortsightedness of science, tend to abound in this genre. *I Am Legend* is a fine example.

Natural Disasters and Terrorism

There's a valley in the overall popularity of zombie films that will be discussed in a later chapter. When zombie films started becoming very popular again after *28 Days Later,* terrorism and natural disasters were very much prevalent in the media, as was anxiety about them. Zombie films, as academics have pointed out, often involve scenarios that resemble extreme outcomes of a terrorist attack, a natural disaster, or an outbreak of illness.

The sort of social commentary in *Dawn of the Dead* is very intellectual. The zombies move slowly enough, in fact, that it's possible to show them as dull-witted creatures aimlessly wandering through a mall. In modern zombie films, starting with *28 Days Later*, the zombie apocalypse is often explosive. It's a fast, brutal thing that doesn't leave much time for reflection, just survival.

In some ways, when zombie films address this, they may be providing a safe outlet for thinking about things that aren't at all pleasant, as do other horror films. Supernatural and realistic horror films allow us to think about topics like death, power, mutilation, disfigurement, and so forth without actually having to endure any hardships.

As was pointed out in a previous chapter, putting together a zombie survival kit is not dissimilar to putting together a preparedness kit for a natural disaster, outbreak of illness, or a terrorist attack. All these scenarios are closely linked, excepting that one is entirely fictional.

In films like *Dawn of the Dead*, there's some reflection on the sociological, philosophical and political aspects of life. In films like *28 Days Later,* there's more of a reaction to a crisis that takes place on the screen. In some regards, these films may even be taken as educational.

On a less philosophical level, the faster zombies also simply appeal to the tastes of the modern filmgoer. They're brutal, deadly and, thus, offer plenty of opportunities for horrific violence and gore.. Slow zombies aren't scary anymore, but fast ones are, and that makes it natural that filmmakers would pick up on that as a way to make more successful films.

As many low-budget filmmakers have found out, it's also possible to do incredible things—like blow up an entire city—using computer effects. This, no doubt, contributes to the explosive chaos of most modern zombie apocalypse scenarios.

The aftermath sometimes makes appeals to notions of national identity and the symbols of it. For instance, in *Shaun of the Dead,* the characters spend an awful lot of time trying to get to The Winchester, the pub where they all hang out. One of the biggest benefits of getting there is that they can trade in their cricket bats and other melee weapons for a functioning rifle, a rare thing in the UK.

In zombie films that take place in the US, on the other hand, expect lots and lots of guns. It makes sense, of course, since there are plenty of guns in the US to grab, and they're a big part of national identity. Even in films from other nations where the characters do manage to get guns, it's not quite the gun show that it is in the US. In films set in the US—everything from comedies like *Zombieland*, to serious films like *Dawn of the Dead*—expect a lot of fancy shotguns and handguns, plenty of hunting rifles and assault rifles, and pretty much anything else that explodes, can be shot, or is otherwise dangerous. In fact, one of the few comforting moments in *Dawn of the Dead* (2004) is the scene where they get into the gun shop and manage to arm themselves to the teeth and beyond.

Just as surviving the natural disaster or plague is important to the amusement park ride that zombie movies tend to be, so too is the idea that the characters retaliate somehow. In US films, expect a pile of spent shells anytime the characters retaliate.

Chapter 5: Story Structure 53

On another, related note, many of these films were influenced by video games; the first-person shooter aspect of them cannot be denied. After the success of *Resident Evil* and *Killing Floor* video game franchises, one should be convinced of the appetite for headshot scenes! *Doom* makes a particularly obvious use of that convention.

The Zom Com

Zom coms (zombie comedies) are very popular. This is not surprising, since both zombie films and comedy films are among the most popular genres. Combining the two seems only natural.

In these films, there are basically two ways that the zombies are portrayed. They may be somewhat sympathetic, such as in *Fido,* or they may be villains, but not necessarily on the level that one sees in a standard zombie film.

Comedy film zombies diverge from horror film zombies in plenty of ways, but they both do about the same thing as far as bringing horrific elements into the story is concerned. In a zombie horror film, the cannibalistic ways of the zombies are all about causing fear and revulsion in the audience. In the comedies, this is usually used to make opportunities for laughter.

Dead Alive is a prime example. This movie is an orgy of bloodshed and gross-out humor. The zombies are certainly dangerous in this film, but the dangers that they present are really just reasons to slice, dice, grind, and lawnmower them out of existence.

Zombie comedies span the gamut, from the sophisticated black humor like *Shaun of the Dead* and some parts of *Zombieland,* to the outright slapstick action in *Return of the Living Dead* series.

Whichever type of comedy you prefer, zom coms offer it. These films rarely have the depth of their more serious kin, of course, though *Zombieland* did give us characters that are worth following and *Shaun of the Dead* had some very sad losses throughout the movie.

There are some themes that zom coms do have in common with more serious films. Here are some of them to watch out for.

Romero's films sometimes play on the concept of zombies evolving and becoming more human, and this has been used in various zombie comedies.

Shaun of the Dead and *Fido* both play on this in unusually comedic ways. In *Fido*, the zombies are basically enslaved. In *Shaun of the Dead*, the ending, of course, makes even more memorable use of this trope.

One of the most famous zom coms, *Return of the Living Dead*, gave us the brain-eating trope that most zombies are associated with these days. It's become a standard joke at this point, even showing up in comical songs about zombies.

The following sections feature several zom coms. Whether or not they're good, of course, depends upon your sense of humor!

Chapter 6

Villains and Heroes of the Zombie Apocalypse

When the end of the world comes, will you be a villain or a hero? Fortunately, zombie films allow us to identify with both. We might find ourselves gravitating toward the stalwart survivors who stick together through thick and thin, or we might see ourselves taking what we can and making it on our own. We might even see ourselves raising a zombie army to do our bidding. No matter how you see it, it's all an acceptable part of a shared fantasy that has roles for people of all dispositions.

The Heroes

The heroes in these films can be of any personality type. They might be gruff, seemingly cold but actually dependable, like the National Guard unit from *Survival of the Dead*. They might be people who just turn out to be good at surviving the zombie apocalypse, and to whom people gravitate out of a need for security, such as Tallahassee in *Zombieland*.

The heroes may also be more serious than either type. When Jim comes through for his friends at the end of *28 Days Later*, he shows as much courage and backbone as anyone who's ever been featured in a zombie film. Likewise, Gerry in *World War Z* keeps coming through for everyone else on the planet and putting his own life at risk in the process.

Here are some of the heroes you're going to see in the films featured in the next section. They are common to many zombie films, and they're great for plot convenience, since these types of characters will have skills that come in very handy during the worst of the zombie apocalypse.

The Cop/Solider

You'll want to stick close to this man or woman. They have the combat skills required to dispense with the hordes of undead, and the leadership skills to keep everyone together. Kenneth in *Dawn of the Dead* (2004) is a fine example of this, as are Peter and Roger in the original.

The Survivalist

This character has managed to figure out not only how to survive the zombie apocalypse, but to thrive in it. Columbus from *Zombieland* is a great example, as is Neville in *I Am Legend*.

The Self-Motivated

Wichita from *Zombieland* starts out this way, but is redeemed as the story goes on. The National Guard members from *Diary of the Dead* also fit this trope, but become steady and authentically good characters in *Survival of the Dead*.

The Altruistic

Dr. Bowman in *Day of the Dead* is a great example of this character type. The world has ended, but she still wants to finish her mission and cure the zombie plague. In some cases, these characters don't last long, so don't get too attached! With all her concern about Chips the dog, Nicole, in the remake of *Dawn of the Dead*, is an example of how this type of character can be a real liability.

The Wise One

This character knows when to take risks and when not to. Sometimes, it might be surprising whom this character turns out to be. Frank in *28 Days Later* knows when to stay and when to go, and saves everyone's skin more than once because of that.

The Infected

The infected hero is a tragic character. Oftentimes, the audience will have a lot invested in them at the time that they turn. At the risk of spoiling some great scenes, some of these characters, when they turn, are likely to break the audience's hearts.

The Villains

The rouge's gallery of zombie film villains is a varied one indeed. There are plenty of types, but here are the most common.

The Vodou Priest

Possibly the most horrific version of this is seen in *The Serpent and the Rainbow*, where the Vodou priest's unearthly power is backed up by the power of a brutal Haitian militia. What makes this even scarier is that, while Vodou priests are the stuff of superstition, the Tonton Macoute were very real and very frightening. Lugosi's aptly named Murder in *White Zombie* is another memorable character along these lines.

The Vodou Priest in a White Lab Coat

Herbert West from *Re-Animator* is a great example of this character, as is Frankenstein from *Day of the Dead*. These characters use the dead to their own ends, but do it with science rather than with Vodou. Neville from *I Am Legend* crosses into this territory a bit with his experiments, but he's certainly not evil.

Military Run Amok

This is a favorite villain of Romero's and is frequently seen in other films as well. In *28 Days Later*, we have one of the most chilling examples of these villains.

How the Vodou Priest Became a Scientist

Over the years, as we'll see in the next chapter, zombie films went from largely supernatural and sometimes downright gothic affairs, to much more science-based horror. This, of course, reflects the trajectory of society.

There's also something of an increased sensitivity toward, and appreciation of, other people's traditions. In films such as *King of the Zombies*—not profiled in this book, as it's not worth seeing—some very ugly racism is on display. As people have given up on the perception that the world is full of savages who need to be civilized, the portrayal of exotic beliefs that involve zombies have changed. In *The Serpent and the Rainbow*, we see a fine demonstration of this very change, as the film doesn't disrespect the Vodou traditions it explores, and gives the audience real reasons to fear those who have acquired power through those traditions.

Chapter 7

Great Directors of the Dead

Some film directors, though they may have careers that involve far more than zombie films, are particularly associated with the genre. The directors that are most associated with creating zombie mythologies are featured here, as well as some film directors who just happened to turn out a great zombie flick among their other works.

George A. Romero

There's probably no director as associated with this genre as is George A. Romero. While he's known for his rather gruesome zombie films, he once said that his scariest film was *Mr. Rogers Gets a Tonsillectomy*. Romero had worked on *Mr. Roger's Neighbourhood*, a children's television show, before shooting the tonsillectomy piece, which was one of many such pieces designed to show Mr. Rogers going through frightening things and coming through all right in the end.

In 1968, Romero made *Night of the Living Dead*. The film was far more than the first zombie film or, at least, the first film that featured creatures that we would call zombies today. *Night of the Living Dead*, featured in the next section, of course, also upped the ante for horror on the screen. Where many other horror films had delivered either more wonder or, sometimes, laughs than anything else, *Night of the Living Dead* was genuinely frightening.

Romero continued to work on his *Living Dead* films throughout his ongoing career. They are listed at the end of this section, along with a rating of 1–5 in terms of how good they are relative to one another. Where zombie films are concerned, it's hard to compare Romero's work with anyone else's, as his was genre-defining.

Romero's films are known for having a lot of social commentary embedded in the story. While some of them, particularly the earlier ones, have many characters who show bigotry against people of other races and immigrants, Romero himself is the son of a Cuban immigrant: his father, who was a commercial artist.

Romero has shot many other films over the course of his career that are far outside the zombie genre. Where zombie films are concerned, however, it's hard to argue that anyone has been as influential as this director.

The Romero *Living Dead* Films and Ratings

Night of the Living Dead (1968): 5/5

Dawn of the Dead (1978): 5/5

Day of the Dead (1985): 4/5

Land of the Dead (2005): 4/5

Diary of the Dead (2008): 3/5

Survival of the Dead (2009): 2/5

Before you skip watching the lower-rated ones, remember that Romero's weakest efforts at zombie films are oftentimes far beyond the strongest efforts of other filmmakers. These ratings are relative to his own films and, compared to *Night of the Living Dead* and *Dawn of the Dead*, it's hard to stand out.

John A. Russo

Russo's career is far more developed as a writer than as a director, though he has directed films. He is most noted for being the writer of—and appearing in, though uncredited—*Night of the Living Dead*, which he co-wrote along with Romero. His and Romero's visions parted following that film. Russo wrote the original novel *Return of the Living Dead*, as well as the novelization of the film of the same name, featured later in the book. He has written several other horror and zombie-themed books, as well as books on the filmmaking process.

Peter Jackson

Before he headed off to Middle Earth, Peter Jackson was well-known as the director of one of the best zom coms around, *Dead Alive* (also known as *Braindead*). Many of his other films were heavily influenced by Romero's work, of which he is a great fan. *Bad Taste*, from 1987, is a low-budget cult classic. His work on *Dead Alive* is still praised for its over-the-top gore and revolting sequences.

Lucio Fulci

Lucio Fulci is an Italian director whose body of work encompasses far more than zombie films. However, he did make one of the most memorable and popular zombie movies of all, *Zombi 2*, which came out in 1979 and is featured later in this book.

Fulci's ventures into zombie films are known for their gut-wrenching gore. Some nations even banned *Zombi 2*. His zombies are distinctive and look more like they just crawled out of a grave than any other director's, complete with worm and maggot infestations, chunks of dirt and grime, and horrifically rotted-away faces.

Zack Snyder

Zack Snyder directed the remake of *Dawn of the Dead*, the first feature film he directed. Before that, he'd directed commercials for some of the most well-known car companies in the world, as well as a host of other films.

Since his debut as a feature film director, Snyder's career has seen him at the helm of action, adventure, and comic book films.

Danny Boyle

Danny Boyle is an award-winning director from England. In addition to his work on *28 Days Later*, he's worked on several highly regarded films outside of the horror genre, including *Slumdog Millionaire,* and *Trainspotting*.

In addition to directing, Boyle writes screenplays and works as a producer.

Not Slumming

Many other directors have made their foray into the zombie genre and, as it is such a popular one, it's certainly not slumming on their part. Indeed, the work of directors such as Danny Boyle on *28 Days Later* show that zombie films, with the right person in charge of the production, can be every bit as dramatic and engaging as the most serious film genres.

Chapter 8

Zombie Films Throughout the Years

Look at the list of films in the second section of this book and you'll see that there wasn't a lot of activity on the zombie front during the 1990s. These films became very popular in the 1970s, continued to be popular through the 1980s, and then sort of dropped off the radar for a while. With the releases of *28 Days Later* and *Dawn of the Dead* however, zombies were literally brought back to life.

Why is this? There are many conflicting theories and, as analytical as one might want to get about it, there's always the possibility that we're just looking at a standard consumer cycle here. People got burnt out on zombies in the 1990s but, with the fast zombie revolution of the 2000s, they were revitalized as frightening film monsters once again.

Dystopia, Mon Amour

Imagine living in a world where people are all equal, unless they prove themselves to be uncommonly good at something. Imagine that how much money you have, what car you drive, or what school you attended were utterly irrelevant to how people assessed you. A true meritocracy, in other words.

For some researchers, zombie films show an evened-out society. In the linked article, the author makes mention of how the zombie apocalypse strips humanity down to its bare essentials. If you're a doctor, that doesn't mean you get a BMW and a membership at the most expensive country club in town. It means that people will try to keep you alive because of what you can do, not worship you because of your financial success. If you happen to be a Vietnam vet who struggled with reintegrating into society and could never leave that war behind, congratulations, your skill set now makes you one of the people that others want to stick with rather than someone who languishes at the fringes of society, underappreciated and misunderstood.

The zombie apocalypse takes us back to our roots, in a way, where we have to survive off the land, and where the character and abilities a person demonstrates counts, and their social status doesn't. In some ways, this is a rather utopian dystopia. Mix this up with the American Dream, as it's commonly known, and you have something interesting. This is a world where hard work and perseverance paying off isn't just a myth.

Those connections to the elites and the most powerful people you made don't matter much when they've all been eaten or zombified. Your BMW? It burns too much gas to be reliable as an escape vehicle. Better grab a sensible compact car. Your stocks and bonds and retirement? There aren't any houses to buy, landlords to rent from, stores to shop at or hospitals to go to, so it's all worthless. It's a massive reboot and, given what was going on in the early 2000s, it's no wonder that these films became so popular.

All that corruption, hate, rage, disfranchisement, hopelessness, poverty, and despair is gone in one outbreak. This is the attractive part of the zombie apocalypse. All that stress is just, suddenly, gone.

The Shifting Natures of Zombies and the Changing Times

During the 1970s and 1980s, zombie apocalypses were slow-moving affairs. They become comical with the *Return of the Living Dead* series. During the 1980s, the zombie films tended to build on the social commentary that Romero wrote into his films, but on a sillier note. Where Romero pointed out that a mall full of zombies isn't much different than a mall full of suburbanites, *Return of the Living Dead* more or less pointed out that punk rockers like to party and that the military and businesses will cover up their tracks if something they do becomes an issue. The social commentary, along with the zombies themselves, became a lighter, more whimsical affair.

Let's look at what might have spurred this. Realize that, like many analyses of why and how films become popular, there's some subjectivity here. Not everyone agrees on why or how zombies drift in and out of popularity.

Night of the Living Dead: Launching a Legend

Night of the Living Dead has been written on extensively already and is featured in the second section of this book. To avoid being redundant, it only needs to be pointed out that the film changed horror movies and the meaning of zombies, and shocked audiences. The copyright flub, no doubt, made it even more popular, as anyone and everyone can show this film whenever and wherever they want without worrying about anyone's rights.

Night of the Living Dead, however, also defined the nature of zombies so well that the trope stuck for many years. Zombies, for over twenty years, remained slow, unintelligent creatures that hungered for human flesh—sometimes brains—and presented the greatest menace when they grouped together. Other than that, they weren't particularly difficult to deal with.

There were plenty of zombie films during the 1970s, though many of them have faded into obscurity over time. *The Dead Don't Die* (1975) and *The Corpse Eaters* (1974) are both examples of this. Nonetheless, there were plenty of titles made during this time, with directors attempting to cash in on what Romero had made so popular. These were almost all "B" films—films that were second-billing to a feature film that was shown at a theater or a drive-in theater.

The thing to remember is that, during the 1960s and 1970s, zombies were generally very frightening, even if they were slow and stupid. This makes them sometimes a threat, but some writers picked up on another potential use for zombies: comedy.

Return of the Living Dead: Making Zombies Comical

During the 1980s, slasher films dominated the world of horror. The violence in films such as *Friday the 13th* and the *Halloween* franchise, for example, led parents conservative regulator groups to protest what they saw as films that presented a threat to the young people who came to see them. Some of these groups claimed to have scientific backing for their points, but this was certainly exaggerated.

Despite the fact that slashers raised some degree of public outcry, audiences—particularly young audiences looking for a thrill—wanted to see violent films. One way to desublimate that which society seeks to sublimate is to cast it in a humorous light.

Enter *Return of the Living Dead*. This film, profiled later in this book, casts zombies in a humorous, slapstick role but keeps the gore intact. There are plenty of nasty kills, bite wounds and so forth in this film, but it lacks the outright cruelty of most slashers.

Chapter 8: Zombie Films Throughout the Years ■ 69

As an indication of how domesticated the zombie was becoming as a monster, consider the video for the Michael Jackson song *Thriller*. In that video, zombies are shown dancing along with the signer. Like Frankenstein's monster and Dracula, zombies were starting to look dated at this time. They were understood to be monsters and dangerous, but not in the same way that slasher villains like Freddy Krueger, Jason Voorhees, or Michael Meyers were. Those characters were genuinely evil and sadistic. Zombies are simply hungry, brainless things that were only dangerous when they appeared en masse.

Some horror films, such as *Creepshow* (1982), incorporated the dead rising from their graves into their plots, but it was oftentimes a different scenario than what one sees in Romero's films. These risen dead were oftentimes purposeful, seeking revenge or, in the case of the aforementioned movie, cake.

One of the reasons that these films became less frightening was possibly due to their relying on established tropes. The dead usually rise from graves, offering a chance to show a clichéd cemetery scene. They shamble about, chase a bunch of teenagers and eat a few people, giving some opportunities for gore. It's very formulaic stuff and, until the 2000s, it stayed within those lines.

Some exceptions include *Hard Rock Zombies* (1985), which managed to make a Nazi/zombie connection, becoming a popular trope in the future. The real exception to how most zombie films were turning out, however, is found in this book in the form of *Re-Animator* (1985).

Re-Animator took a mad scientist, zombies, Frankenstein's monsters, and a reference to H.P. Lovecraft, and bundled all of it into one film.

There is one other horror icon of the 1980s, already mentioned, that has a lot to do with the nature of horror in that time, also incorporating zombie elements: Jason Voorhees.

Voorhees is technically dead. He died as a child, but managed to grow into a hulking brute of a man between the time he died and his resurrection. The first film casts his mother as the killer, making it more of a revenge film. From the second film on, however, except for Part V, it's all about Jason.

Jason has some zombie characteristics. He is to be immune to most anything, barring some sort of special attack, which shifts throughout the films. Headshots don't work on Jason, but there's always some weakness that the protagonists manage to find and exploit, usually after they've been chopped down to one last person remaining.

Voorhees as a zombie is a controversial debate among horror fans. He has many of the characteristics of a zombie, such as being resurrected and hunting down the living, but he has little in common with them in most other ways.

Jason uses weapons, shows some intelligence, and picks targets for reasons other than food. In some ways, Jason is an instance of filmmakers trying to remove the domesticated elements from the zombie and to make them scary again.

The *Friday the 13th* films, however, in every regard other than Jason being undead, are slashers rather than zombie films.

Day of the Dead and *City of the Dead* (1980), the latter another Fulci film, are notably good examples of 1980s zombie films. Along with *Re-Animator*, they provided some evidence that zombies, even in a world where slashers had become the dominant form of horror, could still be frightening. For the most part, however, while one can find zombies in 1980s films, they're just not as scary as they were in the 1960s and 1970s.

While the 1980s don't offer much for those looking for a scary zombie film, the 1990s proved even worse. If you do want to enjoy some zombies that are actually frightening from this decade, look to the foreign films. Of course, *The Serpent and the Rainbow* is a fine zombie film of this era, as is *Pet Sematary*, so there are exceptions.

Chapter 8: Zombie Films Throughout the Years ■ 71

The 1990s: A Game Changes Everything

Perhaps part of the reason that zombie films became less interesting in the 1980s was that, when they weren't horrible, low-budget productions, they still were very predictable. That's a death sentence for any horror-related genre, as the antagonists lose their ability to surprise and shock the audience. The characters in those zombie films tended to be either obvious fodder or obvious protagonists, with a few exceptions.

One way to ratchet up the horror in any genre is to make the audience feel involved. In film, this is done by having sympathetic, interesting characters.

Another way this was done was through a medium that was still coming into its own in the 1990s: video game.

Better hardware, better design, and more grown-up plotlines all contributed to a revitalization of the video game industry in the 1990s. No longer did one have to choose between pumping quarters into an arcade machine or playing on a very low-power machine in their own home. They could load up their PC—or their console—with a game and play for hours, even days, on games that didn't follow the formula of older video games, which typically gave characters around three chances to make it through a challenge before requiring them to start over.

In 1996, *Resident Evil* came onto the market, and it had plenty of zombies. The game was released for the PlayStation console and became a hit.

The zombies in *Resident Evil* were still adhering to the tropes that Romero had started all the way back in the 1960s. They weren't fast or smart, and most of the time you could just avoid them without really having to fight them off.

Resident Evil is the first of a genre of video games called survival horror, which rely heavily on atmosphere, mystery and, oftentimes, being woefully underequipped for whatever you're facing. This is perfect for zombies, and so the association between zombies and video games endured.

Resident Evil had plenty of sequels. Other video games and video game franchises, including *Killing Floor* and *Left 4 Dead* built on this, giving zombies a new life on the small screen, where players sweat out waves of attackers, pick their way through darkened houses, or otherwise encounter zombies or zombie-like creatures.

Zombie films of the 1990s were usually low-budget and not particularly good compared to what came before. While few and far between, there are some great zombie films from the 1990s. *Dead Alive* is one example. There were also various remakes and rereleases of famous films, including a 30th anniversary edition of *Night of the Living Dead*, which really adds nothing to the original film, but might be interesting to die-hard fans.

The zombie renaissance really started with *28 Days Later* in 2002.

The 2000s: The Zombies Get Resurrected

There were zombie films released before *28 Days Later*, including *The Dead Hate the Living!*, which is featured later on. Japan produced some good zombie films during this time. However, none of them really held a candle to what was to come. In 2002, a British film, shot on a limited budget but with plenty of creativity and skill, changed everything.

28 Days Later gave us a serious, believable setup that had nothing to do with the supernatural. It had to do with scientists inventing a horrific virus, well-intentioned but ignorant animal rights activists releasing it into the population, and the chaos and violence that follow. It had one other thing that redefined the genre: fast zombies.

Zombies were starting to look tired and old-fashioned by the time that 2000 rolled around. They were either silly sorts of monsters or

Chapter 8: Zombie Films Throughout the Years

just excuses to include some gut-wrenching gore in a film. Oftentimes, they were treated as pets, continuing the trend that started in the 1990s.

In 2002, however, Danny Boyle tore all of that down. The zombies in *28 Days Later* were terrifying and certainly not what people expected.

The trend would continue, with 2004's *Dawn of the Dead* giving us an updated take on Romero's classic and one that really does live up to the original, but that manages to be its own film at the same time.

Since then, zombies have only become more popular. *The Walking Dead* debuted in 2010 and has become an exceptionally popular TV show, even after it dragged out the zombie apocalypse to span years. Impressive numbers of people tune in every week for more zombie action.

Today's zombie films tend to be darker and more violent than those of the past. While many older zombie films would focus on the zombies eating their kills, or delivering a bit of gore the audience wants, the newer ones tend to concentrate a lot on human suffering and the drudgery of survival. Even starting with *28 Days Later*, this is apparent, as the most dangerous monsters in the film aren't necessarily the zombies.

Zombie comedies have become more sophisticated as well, opening up entirely new roles for these monsters.

However you look at it, zombies have come a long way since they started clawing their way out of their graves in the 1960s, and certainly since Vodou practitioners were making them in the early days of cinema. Today, they're among the most popular of movie monsters and, with constant reinvention, still manage to be scary, which is a great feat for a monster with such a long history at the box office.

Chapter 9

"Real" Zombie Incidents

Just to be clear, there are no documented cases of the dead returning to life and eating the living. Thist hasn't stopped some individuals from playing on the popularity of zombies to make for some real-life fun, however.

There are incidents of people using zombies as examples for educational materials, such as was detailed earlier. There are also instances of people just having a bit of fun with the whole thing, and making it seem like the zombie apocalypse was upon us, or very close to being upon us.

Cambodia Has Zombies!

In April of 2005, the BBC ran an article headlined "Cambodian Troops Quarantine Quan'sul." The story decared that zombies were rising in a small town on the border of Laos and Cambodia.

The story was familiar to anyone who's watched a lot of zombie films. It detailed the effects of a mosquito-borne virus that would kill people in two days—with a 100 percent mortality rate, no less—and would re-start their heart within two hours of the victim dying. The victims were described as being violent when they rose, possibly because of brain damage and a chemical in the blood.

The article even played up a mock disagreement with the US, with Secretary of State at the time, Condoleezza Rice, being mentioned saying that the virus was a biological weapon and that they needed to destroy it. The Cambodians, meanwhile, were quoted as saying that they had gotten samples and that they were going to study it to "increase the quality of life for all."

This article originally ran on April 1, despite the BBC site listing it as April 25. Of course, it was an April Fool's prank, but a pretty good one.

British Humor, Again

The BBC did this one more time, in April 2009, when they made a mock page that reported that zombies were rising in London. This time, they played on real fears of the H1N1 virus, reporting that it had mutated to the H1Z1 virus. The second article went so far as to reference the first article, as reported in Snopes.com. This zombie page isn't available anymore, but the original text that was on the page is reproduced, in part, on Snopes.

Zombies Mosey Into Cowboy Territory

In February 2013, hackers managed to commandeer the Emergency Broadcast System in Great Falls, Montana, and issue a dire warning about the zombie apocalypse. It included the entire Emergency Alert routine, complete with the unmistakable attention-getting noise and a very serious voice alerting viewers to the fact that "civil authorities in your area have reported that the bodies of the dead are rising from the grave and attacking the living."

Videos of the incident are posted on YouTube. The hacks were apparently more widespread than Montana. Everyone seemed to catch on that it was a hoax, however, and no one called the authorities in a panic over the incident. Some, however, did call to ask whether a gun would protect them from the zombies, but did so in jest, according to those reporting on the incident.

The CDC Recommends Zombie Preparedness

As mentioned in previous chapters, the CDC has actually managed to incorporate zombie preparedness into educating people to prepare for real disasters. Dr. Ali Kahn is quoted on the CDC site as saying, "If you are generally well-equipped to deal with a zombie apocalypse, you will be prepared for a hurricane, pandemic, earthquake, or terrorist attack."

You can look at some of the posters that the CDC put out that play on this right here. Horror movies usually don't get much respect, but zombie movies have become such a cultural fixture that even the CDC knows a good opportunity when they see it, and they made great—and really rather fun—use of zombie movie tropes to produce some worthwhile material.

Running a Scam with Zombies

Several bizzare stories involving real, and disturbing circumstances, such as the Florida story involving one man eating another man's face before he was shot by police, gave online scammers a new way to get victims. The scammers put up sites built around a real story, usually promising that by following a malicious link, a reader would get information and updates on the zombie incident.

These were all scams designed to compromise the security on someone's computer, but nonetheless, they show how readily people will bite on a zombie story if they see one in the press.

Remember: zombies do not exist. There are certainly plenty of instances of people engaging in gruesome crimes, but there are no zombie viruses, and Vodou doesn't actually allow people to turn others into zombies.

The stories, however, do make for great movies and, occasionally, for some rather amusing news stories.

Section II: The Films of the Dead

The following section gives synopses and analyses of a range of zombie films from other decades. The material concentrates on the story told in the film, rather than on the story of how the film was made. Some of the latter, however, is included when relevant.

This section contains major spoilers. As was advised before, please watch the films before reading these sections. If you haven't seen the films , the following sections will give away the major plot points and the endings.

Zombie films are oftentimes better the second time around, so, armed with the knowledge in this section, you should get even more out of them on your next time through.

White Zombie (1932)

Director:

Victor Halperin

Starring:

Bela Lugosi

Madge Bellamy

Joseph Cawthorn

Invoking Haitian zombie myths and made before the production code went into effect, *White Zombie* is a cult classic and, according to many critics, a fine film. It is, no matter what one thinks of it, the very first feature-length film with a plot built around zombies. These are traditional zombies, however, so don't expect the hordes of undead to be breaking down doors and lusting after anyone's brains. This film has its own sort of darkness. It featured Bela Lugosi doing what he did best.

The Plot

This film takes place in Haiti, the center of the universe as far as zombie legends go.

Madeleine and Neil plan to be married. They are visiting their friend, Charles, a wealthy plantation owner. Along the way, they meet Murder Legendre, played by Bela Lugosi, who uses Vodou to resurrect the dead to work his sugar mill.

The happy couple makes their way to Charles's plantation, but it soon becomes apparent that Charles has feelings for Madeline. He wants her for himself.

Knowing that Murder might be able to help, Charles visits the Vodou practitioner and solicits his advice. Not surprisingly, Murder recommends zombifying Madeline. Charles agrees.

Charles slips Madeline a potion that Murder provides. She and Neil get married, but the potion kicks in during the dinner following the ceremony and, to all appearances, Madeline drops dead.

Madeline is buried soon after, and Murder and Charles go to her tomb to retrieve her.

Neil enters the tomb not long after the two retrieve the now-zombified Madeline to find that her body is missing. Unsure of what to do, he seeks the advice of Dr. Bruner, who works as a missionary on the island. Bruner knows what has likely happened, as he's familiar with Murder and his ways.

After finding out that Murder possibly resurrected Madeline, the two go to the castle that Murder calls home. There, they confront Charles, who now regrets what he's done. He wants Madeline to be restored to her original state. Murder, being as evil as his name implies, isn't having any of it. Not only that, but he's has already started the process of turning Charles into a zombie.

Murder realizes that Neil has found him out and sends Madeline to kill him. Bruner stops her, however. Madeline, under the control of Murder, heads back to him and Neil and Bruner follow.

During the final confrontation, Murder tries to have his other zombies dispatch with Neil. Once again, Bruner intervenes and knocks Murder unconscious. This breaks his hold over the zombies and they wander away, falling off a cliff.

Charles gets his revenge and pushes Murder off the cliff, killing him, but ends up falling off himself. After Murder is dead, the zombie curse is broken and Madeline is restored.

Eerie in the Extreme

Lugosi is in fine form in this film. Standing under a gas lamp and making his trademark hand gestures, he exercises his power over Madeline, warping her mind to his will. He does the same to the zombies that he has enslaved, thoroughly evil and intoxicated with his own power.

The film is very dark overall, and makes excellent use of shadow. In the sugar mill scenes, the endless squeaking as the slaves work the mill provides the backdrop for the action, and a symbol of the wretched life Murder consigns his slaves.

Murder's castle is wonderfully Gothic. Situated on a high cliff, it provides a natural place for the final action to occur. Overall, this film specializes in shadows and uses them to increase the tension.

This film, because it involves more traditional zombies, doesn't rely on seeing the threat looming at the doorway. Instead, it relies on the supernatural and what lies in the shadows to provide the tension. Add in a particularly sinister Lugosi, complete with crazed, wild eyes, and the very stark settings, and it is quite effective.

The Imperial Angle

There's a fish-out-of-water element to this story. Some writers have described an imperialist angle to it all. As was pointed out, Haitian zombie legends tend to imply that zombification results in slavery, as is the case with Murder's victims, wherein they work on his sugar mill to increase his fortune.

The two protagonists have no idea what they've walked into, but their friend Charles seems to be a part of it as well. A plantation owner, he's practically the definition of imperial society oppressing the natives of the island. He's not quite as evil as Murder but, when he sees something he wants—Madeline, in this case—he's not above using evil to get it.

From the perspective of the natives of the island, the whites were, indeed, imperialists. At the time that this film was made, the US had a military presence on the island. As is the case with most any instance where a nation projects its military force on another nation, the legends of that colonized nation come back home with the soldiers. The legends of the zombies travelled back to the US and this film plays on that.

While there is an imperialist angle here, the film doesn't cast the zombies as the main threat to the protagonists. The threat is enslavement by Murder and, of course, in this sense, the title *White Zombie* can simply be seen as another way of saying White Slavery. A racist term, to be sure—implying that there's an entirely other kind of evil in enslaving *white* people, as compared to everyone else—but one that is really at the heart of what the film presents.

The zombies, unless Murder commands them to be so, aren't really threats at all. The threat doesn't come from being eaten alive by the zombies, but, rather being turned into one, hopelessly enslaved to the wicked Murder forever.

What to Watch For

For any serious zombie fan, there's a lot to take in within the runtime of *White Zombie*.

First and foremost, it's important to note the differences between becoming a zombie in modern films and what it means in this film. In this film, one doesn't truly die and go through resurrection as a zombie. Madeline and the rest of the zombies are alive, but under a spell. This has been addressed in earlier chapters and fits with the traditional depiction of a zombie in folklore. Unlike modern versions of the story, if the zombification is reversed, the affected individual is restored to their former self.

The zombies in this film are also not rotting, shambling corpses. They're human beings who are under mind control, so they look healthy, for all intents and purposes. They may have been compromised mentally, but they're all there physically, and they're not in any danger of falling apart.

In this film, a headshot or a decapitation would result in killing a human being, not stopping a zombie rampage. In fact, it's more desirable to cure the zombies in this film, though one has to get to their master to do that.

Rather interestingly, as it stars Lugosi, this has much in common with the folklore involving vampires, just as it does most of the folklore involving zombies.

In these stories, the zombies are sympathetic characters, as is anyone who has been affected by the evil Vodou master. They've been enslaved, losing all sense of identity and will to make their own decisions. This makes them perfect workers for the brutal sugar mill conditions under which they toil. They never tire and never complain, and, for an evil sort like Murder, this is ideal. The real monster here, in short, isn't an undead corpse, but the utterly soulless and heartless man who controls them.

Appreciating These Zombies

White Zombie is genuinely frightening at times. Some of the folklore surrounding zombies is downright creepy and this story makes great use of that to drive up the tension. People are poisoned without their knowledge, and become zombies before they know what's going on. Poor Neil thinks he loses his wife and, to his horror, finds out that she's actually suffering a fate worse than death.

The music in this film is largely appropriate for the location, giving it an exotic feel that makes it more involving. This film, in fact, has some excellent audio elements, particularly when one considers the time in which it was made. If you're a fan of earlier films, you'll likely appreciate this one. It has all of the features of a horror film of the era, and, aside from being the first zombie film, it's also quite a bit more frightening.

Lugosi might have come off as someone who specialized in cheesy movies, but this film shows that, when he's given the right role, he can be quite convincing. The scenes where he's doing his mind control magic on the zombies are a bit over-the-top and amusing, but when he's delivering dialogue that implies just how powerful he and the Vodou secrets that he's mastered are, he's intimidating.

This film also happens to be in the public domain. This means, of course, that it's one of the many fine films that you can watch completely free and without having to worry about straying into pirate territory. it's available on YouTube any time you want and numerous other sites.

This film is important if you're interested zombie films at all. If your familiarity with the genre starts at *Night of the Living Dead*, you'll get an entirely new type of zombie to enjoy. It's worth taking a look at, for certain, and it doesn't disappoint, even after all these years. It's also less unpleasant than many other zombie films that came out before *Night of the Living Dead*, some of which had racist overtones.

Plan 9 from Outer Space (1959)

Director:

Edward D. Wood, Jr.

Starring:

Bela Lugosi

Tor Johnson

Vampira

Criswell

Plan 9 from Outer Space is considered by many to be the worst film ever made. That might be, of course, a bit hyperbolic, but it is one of those films that's so bad it's good. In fact, this film is likely the one that best defines that description most effectively.

This film, however, does have interesting elements to it regarding zombie treatment, the resurrection of the dead via science, and how it combines various types of horror.

The Plot

The plot of *Plan 9 from Outer Space* can be rather hard to follow but it's a combination of horror, science fiction and, well, Ed Wood.

The film opens up with a monologue by Criswell, a psychic and friend of Ed Wood. He lays out the plot, such as it is. The narration invokes "secret testimony" and the perils of events that take place, which will affect all of us, in the future.

The film takes us to a funeral, where Bela Lugosi and other mourners have gathered for a graveside service for his deceased wife. Next, we're taken to the cockpit of a plane, where two pilots are headed towards Burbank. While one of the pilots is communicating with the air traffic controllers in Burbank, a bright light illuminates the cabin and the pilots observe a UFO. The UFO lands in the graveyard where the funeral is happening, frightening the gravediggers. Vampira—Lugosi's wife in the film—then shows up, risen from the grave, and kills the gravediggers.

The film contains several sequences put together from footage that Wood shot of Lugosi before his death. As Lugosi walks out of his home, a narrator explains that Lugosi's character has no desire to live anymore after the death of his wife. Lugosi walks off-screen. We hear a car crash and a scream, and then see ambulances.

At the old man's funeral, one of the mourners finds the bodies of the gravediggers, which brings the police to the scene to investigate. Inspector Clay, played by Tor Johnson, leads them. They investigate the graveyard and look for clues as to who committed the murder.

One of the pilots of the plane, Jeff Trent, lives near to the graveyard with his wife, Paula. In the next scene, we see Jeff lamenting that the military is keeping him from telling anyone about the UFO he saw. As he and his wife discuss the matter, another UFO flies over, knocking them and the furniture on the deck to the floor.

Soon after, the old man—no longer played by Lugosi, who was dead when these sequences were shot—is resurrected. He and Vampira run into Inspector Clay as he investigates the graveyard. He tries to shoot them, but they're not fazed and kill him.

A compressed time sequence follows, in which UFOs are seen in many major cities. The military tries to repel them, but the weapons prove ineffective. A government conspiracy story is introduced, with a new character, Colonel Thomas Edwards, Chief of Saucer Operations, explaining to an underling that the UFOs have been visiting for some time. The government initially tried to communicate with them, but they got no response, so they started shooting at the UFOs. The aliens have already wiped out a town—a small town, he notes—and the government covered it up.

We next meet the aliens. Eros is the head of the invasion force, and has instituted Plan 9. Plan 9 involves the resurrection of the dead by manipulating their pineal and pituitary glands.

Paula is soon attacked by the old man, Vampira, and Inspector Clay, after Eros orders his underlings to have one of the resurrected dead invade someone's house. She ends up running into the graveyard, collapses of fright, and is rescued by a passerby.

Meanwhile, the government has figured out a way to translate messages sent by the aliens. The aliens are trying to stop humankind from destroying the entire universe, but humanity couldn't understand their purpose until now. Colonel Edwards is sent to California to investigate the strange happenings at the graveyard.

The police are still trying to figure out the murders at the cemetery and are interviewing Trent and his wife. The old man ambushes one of the officers, who tries to shoot him. Of course, it doesn't do anything, but the aliens kill the old man, turning him into a skeleton with their ray guns.

Trent and three of the policemen investigate the graveyard while Paula and another officer wait in the car. The Inspector Clay zombie kidnaps Paula and takes her back to the ship. The officers and Trent see the ship and go to investigate.

Trent and the police confront the aliens in the ship. Eros goes off on a rant about how stupid human beings are and how they're going to blow up the universe by exploding the particles that make up sunlight. He gives a long speech involving a gas can and a trail of gasoline as an analogy, saying that the chain reaction will blow up every star in the universe and destroy it.

The two officers outside the ship find Paula, who is being held by Inspector Clay. They ambush him with a post. Eros turns off the ray that's controlling Inspector Clay, and the officers rescue Paula.

Trent and Eros get into a fight. His assistant, Tanna, tries to radio for help, but the two battling men destroy all the equipment on the ship and set it on fire. The officers and Trent get off the ship and Tanna flies away, the ship ablaze. After the ship explodes, Vampira and

Inspector Clay are both turned into skeletons. The film ends with a closing narration by Criswell.

Technology and Its Perils

As discussed earlier, zombies originally came from Vodou mythology. In this film, we see among the first instances where they are portrayed as coming back to life due to entirely scientific means.

While this has been done in the past—*Frankenstein*, after all, was about resurrecting the dead via science—*Plan 9 from Outer Space* casts science as the bad guy. It both threatens to destroy the entire universe and can be put toward resurrecting the dead to serve as weapons of terror.

While *some may regard Plan 9 from Outer Space* as the worst film ever made, it's hard to ignore the fact that there is real ambition on display. In fact, this film actually mirrors some of what are generally regarded to be the best films of the time. It doesn't exactly reach their level, but it does make an attempt.

For one thing, the aliens give a rather dire warning. Though it's couched in some very silly language, the aliens warn that humanity is going to destroy itself and the entire universe. This is pretty close to what goes on in *The Day the Earth Stood Still*, which is regarded as a great film. Resurrecting the dead is proof of the power that the aliens wield, so there's some gravity to what they're saying. At least, there would be in a better film.

Since the topic is zombies, however, let's look at the zombies in this film and what makes them tick.

Space Zombies

Combining science with resurrecting the dead is, of course, nothing new, but there's an interesting treatment of it here in that the aliens are deliberately "weaponizing" the dead. In *Night of the Living Dead*, contamination from space leads to the zombie resurrection, but it's not a deliberate move on the part of an alien intelligence. It most certainly is here.

The zombies in this film display behaviors that will become standard operating procedure for zombies for decades to come. They have the slow, menacing walk and the expressionless faces. They're not rotted or decaying like zombies in later films, but they've only been dead a short time.

Interestingly, Lugosi never really plays a zombie in this film. This is actually a trope called a Fake Shemp, in which a stand-in is used for an actor who is not available at the time. This particular example is considered one of the most ineffective and unconvincing ever put on film, which fits with the rest of the film's reputation. The stand-in was a chiropractor who treated Wood's wife. Wood believed that, with his cape over his face, he looked enough like Lugosi to pull it off, though the result was amusing, to say the least.

Lugosi was most associated with gothic horror, particularly with Dracula. In fact, his Dracula cape—or an imitation of it—is what makes it possible for Wood to try to pull off the Fake Shemp in this film. Lugosi is, of course, the antagonist in *White Zombie,* where he

Films of the Dead

commands zombies of the more traditional sort. This film, however, resurrects the dead in a more modern sci-fi/horror crossover.

The zombies in this film, though they're intended to be the real scare, are really not much to worry about. You'll notice that they move slowly enough that just about anyone could run away from them without any trouble. Bullets don't seem to faze them but, then again, no one seems to attempt a headshot, either.

The zombies in *Plan 9 From Outer Space* are something of a cross between later zombies, such as Romero's, and the earliest zombies in film and mythology. They're directly under the control of their creators, just as the zombies resurrected by a Vodou priest would be. They're not magical zombies, however, making them more similar to modern zombies, which are usually resurrected by a virus, technology, or something else that falls firmly in the realm of science.

As far as threats, go, they're too slow to be as frightening as the fast zombies that became popular in the early 2000s. There are also too few to be as frightening as Romero's zombies, which overwhelmed people by sheer numbers.

Overall, the zombie menace in this film is more gothic in its horror than anything else. It's all about atmosphere and, had there been more of a budget behind this film, it might have actually been a really interesting contrast and combination of gothic and sci-fi horror.

Enjoying These Zombies

Plan 9 from Outer Space is easy enough to enjoy, particularly given its reputation. Clearly, it isn't a good film, but it genuinely is so bad it's good. At some level, the flaws make it a lot of fun and the resurrecting-the-dead element is a big part of that. Watching Vampira, not-Bela Lugosi, and Tor walk around with their arms outstretched with cheesy Halloween-zombie expressions is genuinely hilarious.

There is something more to this film, however. People love this film. There are several versions of it out there, including a colorized one. The colorized one had several changes made as the result of a contest. The winners of the contest, among other things, got their name added to a gravestone and got to decide that Eros should turn green for a second after he gets punched by Trent.

Whether you go for the black and white or the color version of this film, it's worth seeing. There are plenty of bad zombie films out there, but this one shows that a film doesn't have to be good to be enormously entertaining. The UFOs look like the toys that they are. The special effects shots are atrocious. The plane cockpit has plywood controls, and, in the new version, with the aspect changed, you can clearly see that Trent is reading the script, which is sitting in his lap as he delivers his lines.

What works about this film is that it almost ascends to the level of a parody of better films. It has the dire warnings for humanity given in *The Day the Earth Stood Still*. It has the same science/zombie connection that we see in *Night of the Living Dead*. And it has one of the worst examples of trying to include an actor in a film even though they couldn't make it to the set (on account of being dead, in Bela's case).

The 'worst movie ever made' title comes from the book "The Golden Turkey Awards" by Michael Medved and Harry Medved. The title stuck, though there are certainly films out there worse than this and far less entertaining. If you want to watch a film with zombies, UFOs, government conspiracies, someone doing an awful job of Fake Shemping, Bela Lugosi and stock footage galore, there's only one place to go: Ed Wood. Say what you want about the film, but it's memorable, a lot of fun, and worth watching, which is a lot more than you can say about some of the films that critics lavish praise upon.

This film is in the public domain, so you can watch it to your heart's content without paying a dime. You can check it out on YouTube or download it from numerous different sources.

The Last Man on Earth (1964)

Director:

Ubaldo Ragona

Sidney Salkow

Starring:

Vincent Price

Franca Bettoia

The Last Man on Earth is based on the book *I Am Legend* by Richard Matheson. This book also provides the basis for the film of the same name featured later in this book. This film, however, is a far different than the recent Will Smith picture. It features Vincent Price at his best, the titular last man on earth, and it mixes up various horror villains in a memorable way.

The Plot

Price plays Dr. Robert Morgan. The action takes place in 1968, four years after the film was released.

In this future, Morgan goes through a monotonous routine every day. On the day the movie starts, he has coffee and orange juice for breakfast, and then spends some time trying to radio to someone, anyone, on an amateur radio setup.

Civilization has been brought down by a plague that claimed Morgan's family, in addition to the rest of humanity, for all Morgan can tell. After someone dies of this plague, they're resurrected as a sort of combination zombie/vampire. They behave as zombies do in most films, slow-witted, and deadly if they manage to overwhelm their victims. They have the classic weaknesses that one would expect of vampires, however, including aversions to sunlight and garlic. Morgan spends his days killing the undead off wherever he can find them, and the nights barricaded in his house.

Unlike most movie zombies, these ones talk, calling "Morgan! Come out!" from outside his door. He largely ignores them at night; they're too stupid to find their way in and he uses what he can to repel them from the house.

Morgan's daughter and wife died of the plague, but he was unaffected. He believes his immunity is the result of being bitten by a bat when he was abroad. His theory is that the bite acted as a vaccine, exposing him to enough of the bacteria that caused the vampire/zombie resurrection to build immunity to it, but not enough of the bacteria to actually kill him.

When the plague was in full swing, vast burning pits were made to dispose of the dead. Morgan couldn't bring himself to burn his wife in one, so he tried to bury her in secret. She came back to him, however, and Morgan figured out that the only way to kill off the vampire/zombies was by driving a wooden stake through their hearts. He's been doing as much to a great number of vampire/zombies since civilization fell.

Morgan finds a dog and make friends with it, but it proves to have been infected. He's forced to kill and bury it. He then meets a woman named Ruth. He suspects that she's infected, as well, and tries to test her by exposing her to garlic. She manages to avoid Morgan finding out, until he sees her injecting herself.

Ruth and a group of fellow survivors have figured out a way to keep the infection from killing them, but they cannot cure it. If they stop treating themselves with the medicine they've developed, they quickly revert to vampire/zombies.

The survivors are aware of Morgan and, as it turns out, he's killed people that they considered to be alive. They sent Ruth to check out Morgan and his activities.

Morgan decides that he could help Ruth and gives her a transfusion. It works, and Ruth is cured of the infection. Ruth's compatriots want to rebuild civilization and, with this new revelation, it seems hopeful, but they attack before Morgan can tell them.

Morgan flees from Ruth's group. They chase him down to a church and kill him, driving a spear through him and leaving him on the altar. He calls them freaks and dies.

Bleaker than Bleak

This is not a high-budget film, but it is quite effective. It makes the best of the fact that Morgan is, after the sun goes down, trapped in his home. He sleeps listening to jazz music while the vampire/zombies bang on the door, yell for him to come out and break things outside.

Vincent Price is also very effective in this film. He looks genuinely anguished a great deal of the time and does a great job of straddling the line between boredom and insanity. He's isolated, desperate and, aside from civilization collapsing, he's also lost his family and that's clearly hurt him worse than anything else. He even visits a church, at one point, trying to find some sort of comfort in at least the trappings of civilization. He manages to get in a nap at the church and ends up sleeping too long, having to fight his way through a horde before he can get back to his car. Fortunately, the vampire/zombies are not particularly effective and he manages to do so.

Unfortunately, getting away just means getting back to his lonely house, where he spends the night smoking and watching home movies. There's no future for this man, and that's what really drives this film.

Enjoying These Zombies

The creatures in this film are combinations of vampires and zombies, though this is different from the book on which the film was based. In the book, the creatures that rise from the dead are far more like traditional vampires.

Because they do have the vampire traits, these zombies have the unusual quality of being dispatched by a wooden stake to the heart. Shooting them in the head would apparently do no good.

There's another element to this film that differentiates it quite a bit from others of its type. In this film, it's implied that the vampires/zombies are going to rebuild society. In fact, they've already decided that Morgan is a murderer, as the affected individuals could realistically have their condition managed.

Morgan is really a legend, as the novel's title suggests. There's no one like him alive on Earth at the time the movie starts, and Earth appears to be moving on without him. There's a subtext here of things changing and of Morgan being the last man holding onto the old way of life, which isn't feasible anymore due to the bacterial infection that started the entire plague.

Despite Morgan's awful fate, there is hope that society will be rebuilt but in the zombies' eyes, Morgan is the threat and has to be eliminated.

Don't Underestimate This Film

This is a low-budget film, mostly shot in Italy, and at times, it shows. Don't let that put you off. *The Last Man on Earth* is a good film, and one that's often overlooked as one of the better zombie films out there.

Consider what this film avoids. It doesn't rely so much on the zombie threat to drive the horror, but instead on what's happening to the protagonist because of it. Rather than the film's plot logically resulting in the nadir of society, there's the implication that society will simply change, as the survivors will figure out how to treat their condition and live despite it, building something new from the ruins of society.

Vincent Price tends to get the short shrift where his acting is concerned as well. He can be melodramatic and, in some roles, that was particularly well suited to his character. In this one, he's convincing. He's old enough to be believable as an accomplished doctor, avoiding one of the pitfalls of modern movies wherein clearly young actors portray characters that would have needed decades of experience to get to the displayed level of proficiency in their fields. It's easy to believe that Morgan could have been an accomplished physician.

Price also drives home the point that it's not clear what his character is even fighting for. His family is gone, his friends are gone, his whole community is gone—yet he keeps on fighting. For what? No one is on the other end of the radio when he tries to call out. No one is in the stores he visits when he goes scavenging for supplies and on zombie-killing excursions. He's a legend, as the name of the book implies, but he's only legendary because he's the last man standing and, without the new crop of humanity to come up and replace him, there wouldn't even be anyone to recognize him for what he is.

This film is worth watching. It's not the standard zombie film, of course, but the vampires are zombie-like enough that fans of the genre will appreciate it. The vampire references, in fact, seem out of place in this film, as the mobs outside Morgan's door behave much more like zombies.

There is a colorized version of this film, and the black and white is widely available as well. It's in the public domain, so you can watch it on YouTube for free, and it's well worth the time investment.

Night of the Living Dead (1968)

Director:

George A. Romero

Starring:

Duane Jones

Judith O'Dea

Judith Ridley

Karl Hardman

Marilyn Eastman

This is it. Of all the zombie films you'll read about in this book, *Night of the Living Dead (NOTLD)* is the most influential. This film is part of the National Film Registry in the Library of Congress. This film influenced so many other films that it's hard to imagine the current state of horror without it. This film and its legacy have launched many successful franchises and have created an entirely new mythology that has captivated America over the years.

The zombie apocalypse, the headshot, kill it with fire, boarding up the house, survivor panic; they all start here, in a low-budget black and white film that never once uses the name "zombie" to refer to what are among the most iconic horror movie villains in the world.

The Plot

Barbara and Johnny are brother and sister and have headed out to the country to visit their father's grave. While they're at the cemetery, Barbara becomes uncomfortable and Johnny utters one of the most famous movie lines in history:

"They're coming to get you, Barbara."

They *are* coming to get Barbara, and the action starts soon after. Barbara is the first person that we see being attacked by one of the living dead. Johnny steps in, but he's no fighter. He loses his balance and falls headfirst onto a gravestone, leaving poor Barbara alone.

Barbara gets to the car, but the zombies are hot on her heels and she crashes the vehicle. Barely managing to escape, she makes it to a seemingly abandoned farmhouse. However, the farmhouse isn't abandoned; it's already been attacked and become a charnel house. Barbara's already significant trauma is increased when she sees a half-eaten corpse.

She tries to flee, but runs right into more of the creatures. Fortunately, Ben, who becomes the main protagonist of the film, arrives and gets her back into the house and to safety.

Ben is resourceful and smart and immediately begins fortifying the house. He doesn't have a plan yet, but he clearly values staying alive. He tries to reach Barbara, but she's so traumatized that she's unable to do anything but panic.

In the basement, a young couple, as well as a married couple and their daughter have taken shelter from the living dead. The daughter, Karen, was bitten by one of the zombies and is falling ill.

The husband, Harry, immediately begins an argument with Ben. He believes that they're all safest in the cellar and demands that Ben and Barbara join them. Ben disagrees, reasoning that, if the horde breaks into the home they will be trapped in the cellar without any means of escape. Tom, the male half of the young couple, agrees with Ben and helps Ben to make sure that the house is well-fortified.

The group begins trying to discern what's going on. All the radio reporters know is that there is a wave of mass murder and the entire East Coast is being affected. Ben manages to find a television and, from that reporting, finds out that it's not mass murder. It's the dead—they're coming back to life and they're apparently some sort of ghoul when they do come back, feeding on living human beings.

All the authorities can figure out is that the likely cause of the resurrections is a form of radiation detected on a probe that recently returned from Venus. When the government detected that the probe was contaminated, they blew it up in orbit and, apparently, that radiation reached the Earth and caused the dead to start rising from their graves.

Ben and the rest of the group decide to make a break for Willard, a town located not too far away that has medical help for Karen. Ben's truck is low on gas, but the farmhouse has a gas pump. Unfortunately, there's a throng of dead between the house and the gas pump.

Harry, realizing that Ben has a good plan, helps Tom and Ben get to the pump by tossing Molotov cocktails at the living dead to keep them away. Tom's girlfriend, Judy, goes out to help them.

While they are filling up the truck, Tom spills some gasoline, and it catches fire. He and Judy are both killed when the truck explodes, but Ben makes it back to the farmhouse.

Harry freezes and doesn't open the door for Ben when he returns. Ben makes it back into the house and makes sure Harry regrets it.

Ben checks the news again and finds out that the only definite way to kill off one of the living dead is to shoot it in the head or to burn it. Groups of armed men have gotten together to kill off the living dead wherever they find them.

The tension between Ben and Harry comes to a head when the power is cut. They struggle and, eventually, Ben shoots Harry. Karen has died from her injuries and Harry makes it down to the cellar and dies by his daughter. Helen, Harry's wife, and Barbara are attacked by the living dead, who break into the house. Helen makes it back down to the basement but, by that time, Karen has resurrected and is feasting on her father. Karen attacks her mother and kills her, stabbing her to death. Ben makes it down to the basement and kills Harry and Helen, who are already coming back to life. Barbara gets eaten by the living dead.

Ben survives the night and goes to the window after he hears shooting. A posse has shown up and are clearing out the horde of living dead. He peeks out the window and one of the posse shoots him, killing him instantly. He's tossed on the fire with the rest of the dead bodies.

What Was That?

For a modern movie fan, the description above probably sounds like a standard zombie film. A bunch of people have to barricade themselves into a house to survive a zombie assault. Among them, there is a leader, an antagonist, an infected person, three victims and a right-hand man for the leader character. They fight off the zombies by securing their position and using guns and fire as weapons, and improvising when they have neither.

Imagine, however, seeing this film in 1968. There had never been anything like this before. Consider how revolutionary it really was.

To start with, it's impossible to ignore the fact that this was one of the few American films of the time with a black protagonist. What's more, the black protagonist is leading a group of white people, which makes it even more unusual. Tom, the young man, has no trouble seeing Ben as a leader, as Ben clearly has the best head on his shoulders and seems to be the best fighter of the group, to boot. This makes the film even more enjoyable, in many regards, considering

Films of the Dead

that it came out when the battles over equal rights for African Americans were very violent and very common.

As for the horror elements, they're horrific, to be sure. The living dead are not rubber monsters, cheesy UFO-flying aliens, or dramatic, gothic horror villains. They're relentless killing machines that devour the living. They're rotting, decayed, shambling and, aside from headshots or fire, essentially unstoppable. Their visages are twisted mockeries of the living. In short, they must have scared audiences of the time to their cores and, according to the reviews featured in the first chapter of this book, they did.

The horror goes further than that, however. This is one of the first films that gives us the modern zombie apocalypse in all its glory. The news chatters away about how no one knows or understands what's really going on. Posses pop up and provide the only way of dealing with the situation. The group at the center of the action want to get to shelter, but that's no small trick in a situation where even getting out of the house means taking on the undead.

It's important to remember that the zombies in this film aren't referred to by that name. They're really ghouls, if one's being technical about it, and the film refers to them being reactivated, rather than reanimated, at one point. Part of what makes this film so effective is what the characters, and the audience, don't know.

This Never Happened Before

In most modern zombie films, the setup is cursory. All that needs to take place is the characters becoming aware that the dead have risen. Once that's established, the characters and the audience know that there are some basic ground rules. Don't get bitten, don't get cornered, don't split off from your group, and aim for the head. When *NOTLD* came out, people had no idea about any of these things.

It takes exposition during the film to explain to the audience how the undead can be dispatched. There's no real precedent for any of what goes on, and that means that the characters—and the audience—are really in unknown territory. That makes all the difference in this film.

Taking a cue from this film, other zombie movies have managed to deliver on the thrills and chills, but to understand how this film must have played out to the original audiences, the element of the unknown is key. Watching a modern zombie film—when one knows what to expect—compared to seeing this one when it first came out, is like comparing a ride on a roller coaster to a ride on a runaway train. One is safe and designed to offer chills, the other is just out of control and a complete wild card.

What's truly remarkable about *NOTLD* is that, decades and many movies later, it still works. It's still one of the best zombie movies out there. Watch it for the experience of seeing what terrified audiences when it first came out, but also watch it because it's just a great film all around. It started the zombie trend, but it also defined what really works in these films and that hasn't changed all that much over the years.

Enjoying These Zombies

These are the original zombies—even though they're not called that in the film—so anyone who loves these films should enjoy *NOTLD*. This film, within the space of its 97-minute runtime, fully defines most of the tropes that would come to be staples of zombie movies forever after.

It's easy to overlook the fact that little zombie lore existed at the time this film was made. For instance, there was no precedent stating that zombies had to eat people. That was something that the filmmakers came up with when trying to figure out what the most shocking thing the monsters could do. In earlier films, zombies just kill people, for the most part, or work as slaves. In some films—*Plan 9 from Outer*

Films of the Dead

Space, notably—the zombies mostly just shamble around and look menacing.

The film is also great for its protagonist. Duane Jones, who played Ben, was chosen for the lead simply because he was the best actor at the audition. While this film is notable for being important in the horror genre, it's also notable in that the filmmakers just chose the best actor and disregarded his race, which is really quite remarkable for the time.

The creatures are referred to as ghouls in the film, which is actually a more accurate term, given their nature and behavior. They might be regarded as the original zombies these days but, in the time that this film was made, a zombie still had more to do with Vodou than anything else in the minds of most audiences. "Living Dead" fits nicely, as well.

There's one other thing that makes this film truly great: it belongs to everyone. At the time the film was released, it was necessary to put a copyright notice on anything that one wanted to secure rights to. Unfortunately for the filmmakers, they forgot to put a copyright notice on this film—originally titled "Night of the Flesh Eaters"—and, thus, the film went into the public domain immediately. You can watch it on Archive.org and any of a number of other sites, including YouTube, and there's no piracy involved. If black and white doesn't appeal to you, there's a colorized version available on YouTube as well. This is everyone's film, though one must feel a bit bad for the filmmakers, who lost tens of millions of dollars because of a simple printing error. There's a subtitle file with the download from Archive.org, as well, which is a good idea to get, since this is a low-budget film with mono audio mastering.

Night of the Living Dead, if you're not that familiar with zombie films, will provide you with all the introduction you need. If you're already a zombie fan and haven't seen this film, you're most certainly missing out.

Horror Express (1972)

Director:

Eugenio Martin

Starring:

Christopher Lee

Peter Cushing

Telly Savalas

Helga Line

George Rigaud

Victor Israel

Horror Express is among the public domain films that are actually quite good and that deserve a viewing. This isn't cutting-edge cinema and it has its tedious points, but the presence of Cushing and Lee, two legends of mid-20th century horror, make it well worth seeing for anyone who likes films of the era.

The Plot

The action in this film takes place on the Trans-Siberian Express as it speeds across Russia in 1906. The main character is Alexander Saxton, a professor of anthropology who has been studying what appears to be an evolutionary missing link that he discovered in China. He has a professional rivalry with Doctor Wells, but the two are not enemies, and seem friendly for the most part.

The action begins quickly, with a body found at the train station. The eyes of the corpse are completely white.

A priest, Father Pujardov, is among the passengers. He has reservations about the remains that Saxton is transporting, believing them to be evil.

The rivalry between Wells and Saxton gives us our first view of the creature in the crate. Wondering why Saxton is so secretive about what he's found, Wells manages to get access to the contents of the crate, but has a porter do the work for him. The contents of the crate turn out not to be dead and the creature inside kills the porter and then gets free.

With the shark now in the water, the tension mounts. The creature goes on a killing spree, leaving each victim looking like the dead body at the train station, with no irises or pupils. Doctors examine the dead bodies and discover that whatever killed them was also affecting their brains, sucking the memories and knowledge out of their minds.

Under further examination, the doctors discover that they can access the last things the victims saw by autopsying their eyes and extracting a fluid from them. The fluid reveals strange images, including images of Earth long in the past and an image of the planet apparently taken from space.

The doctors are not narrow-minded and, given what they see, they deduce that the creature cannot be of this world and that, in fact, it must not even have a body, moving from victim to victim. The creature has apparently moved into a fresh victim and, after he figures this out, the Father decides to become a follower of the creature.

It's not long before the Russians send the military to investigate, in the form of Captain Kazan. Played by Savalas, Kazan does not seem like a man to cross. He believes that there are rebels on the train. He begins his investigation, but after Saxton manages to show him someone possessed by the alien by switching off the lights—making the man's eyes glow—the Captain is convinced. The creature has a plan, moving from passenger to passenger devouring their useful knowledge and memories, trying to escape the planet and get home.

The Captain shoots the current host, but the alien transfers to the Father. The passengers get to the freight cars and the Father gets the best of the Captain, all the men that accompanied the Captain, and a Polish count. Saxton manages to rescue everyone.

Saxton also figures out that the creature is trapped in its current host when in the presence of bright light. He sets up part of the train with bright lighting to protect everyone. He reasons that the creature can jump from organism to organism, no matter how primitive, and the combination of the images of prehistoric Earth and the shot from outer space prove that it has been alive for a very long time.

The creature, confronted by Saxton, reveals that it's from another galaxy, that it came with others like itself, and that it's a form of energy. The creature wants to get home and offers to exchange some of its knowledge for not being killed. When given the chance, however, it inhabits another corpse and attacks Saxton. The creature's powers prove to be even deadlier as the film climaxes.

Slowly, the corpse of the count starts to rise, prompting Saxton to shoot it with a shotgun and get to the caboose. The whole lot of the corpses then begin to rise, attacking Saxton and the countess as they try to make their way through the train. Saxton shoots them down at first, eventually resorting to picking up the dead captain's scimitar and fighting them hand to hand.

The pair makes it to safety, but a crowd of zombies marches through the train, hot on their heels. Meanwhile, Wells begins detaching the caboose from the train, but Saxton and the countess make it to safety just in time. The two scientists free the caboose before the zombies can make it to them, all under the red-eyed stare of the creature.

The train station gets an order to stop the express, which means killing everyone on it. Reasoning that war must have broken out, the station operators comply and switch the tracks. The group in the back, however, manages to unhitch the caboose before it spills over a cliff with the rest of the train. The main part of the train plunges into the snow, crashing and burning up, while the caboose stops just at the edge, affording the survivors a view of the carnage below.

The survivors leave the caboose as the train burns away below them. A final shot shows the train engulfed in flames and a receding shot of the Earth.

Another Reason to Explore the Public Domain

This film is not of the same caliber of *Night of the Living Dead*, but it is quite good. Like that film, it is in the public domain and free to watch on many different sites, no piracy involved. We all own this film, basically.

The film makes great use of the train setting and really plays up having some areas of the screen shadowed in impenetrable black. The effects are simple but gruesome, particularly because of how they focus so much on the eyes.

This film has more of a traditional zombie feel to it, with the alien taking the place of the Vodou priest. Science, in this case, is both the reason for the creature escaping and the only means for the passengers to figure out what's going on.

Wells and Saxton are good-guy scientists and they are exceptionally skilled at investigation. Watching Cushing and Lee play off of one another is always a good time, and this film doesn't disappoint in that regard. Savalas is a great choice to play the Cossack captain. His intimidating nature suits the role well, and, even at his cruelest, there's a weird joy that comes through, indicating that he's having a good time. This making the scenes somewhat amusing.

The alien is effective. There are shades of *The Thing* in the story, of course, but that doesn't detract from the plot at all. IIt makes good use of paranoia, wherein no one is sure who the good guys and bad guys really are.

This film doesn't become a fully-fledged zombie film until the very end, but when it does, the payoff is excellent.

Enjoying These Zombies

The zombies in this film start out as variations on the classic Vodou zombie. They're under the control of another force that exploits them for their memories and their knowledge. The twist is that the force is also using the zombies to avoid detection by the human beings. Seeing the tremendous power of the creature, the Father bows down to it, becoming something of a willing slave to the Vodou master, or what passes for Vodou master in this film.

The zombie attack isn't particularly gory at all, save for their bloodied eyes and lack of pupils or irises. They reach out, move slowly, and aren't shown to be very strong or agile, but there are enough of them to make the close quarters of the train genuinely frightening. The way that the film makes use of those dark shadows only adds to the overall sense of menace.

This film is worth seeing. It's been featured on many different hosted horror programs, an it's in the public domain. It does move slowly at times and, of course, the level of gore that a modern viewer would expect in a film of this sort isn't there. For atmosphere, great actors and an interesting twist on the reanimated dead, however, this film delivers. You can go check it out on YouTube right now.

Let Sleeping Corpses Lie (1974)

Director:

Jorge Grau

Starring:

Juan Cobos

Sandro Continenza

This film was released under more than a dozen different titles over the years, so you may well find it under another name. It takes place in England, but most of what appears on screen was actually produced in Italy. This film combines the fear of pollution, serial killers, and zombies into one gruesome whole, and offers some of the best of what '70s zombie films were known for.

The Plot

The film starts with George, the owner of an antique store in Manchester, taking a trip on his bike. He is on his way to help renovate a house and takes with him an antique statue that he plans on selling.

As he's waiting for a fill-up at a gas station, a woman parked in front of him accidently puts her car in reverse instead of in drive and wrecks his bike. It does enough damage that the wheel needs to be replaced. George demands that the woman, Edna, give him a ride to the Lake District in exchange for having ruined his motorcycle. She agrees, and the two take off together.

Edna is going to see her sister and seems to be in a rush, but isn't clear about why. She and George agree that George will take her car on to the Lake District and she'll send someone to get it after George drops Edna off at her sister's house.

Along the way, the two get lost. George fjords a river and heads to a farm to get directions. When he arrives, he sees a man in a field using a curious silver device that looks like a parabolic dish that the man. He is pointing it at the ground. The man, and the crew with him, are from the Department of Agriculture. They'd developed a device to help fight off insects and other vermin. It uses radiation to make them extremely aggressive, causing them to start killing one another.

Edna, back at the car, sees a man wandering around by the river. He comes after her, half shambling but still fast enough to be a threat. She manages to get to George, but the man vanishes.

We then meet Edna's sister, Katie. She has a bad heroin problem and is married to a photographer, Martin, with whom she's arguing. While Martin goes out to take some pictures, the man that attacked Edna shows up and attacks Katie. She makes it back to Martin, and Martin attempts to kill the man, hitting him in the head with a rock. The man is incredibly strong, however, and Martin dies in the attack. George and Edna arrive at the house as Katie gets back.

They report the murder to the police, but the sergeant seems determined to blame it on one of the three protagonists. George cannot go on in his journey because of the investigation, but he steals the film out of Martin's camera and has it developed.

George and Edna go to the Old Owl Hotel, which actually has an old owl living in the lobby. Katie, in the process of kicking heroin, cannot deal with the stress of the murder and is sent to the hospital to recover.

George and Edna find out that the man who attacked them matches the description of a man who used to live by the river and who drowned. The pictures form Martin's camera don't return anything of use. The police sergeant isn't amused at all by the fact that George took the film and had the pictures developed and has Edna and George tailed by one of his officers.

George and Edna shake the cop tailing them and head to the graveyard to investigate on their own. They're soon discovered by the zombie, who begins resurrecting the other dead bodies.

The police officer finds them and rescues them from being pulled into a pit of zombies. They all take shelter in a house, barricading the doors and trying to figure out what to do. Guns don't seem to work on the zombies, but the police officer decides that he'll try to make it to his radio, which he dropped outside, so he can send for help.

As he makes a dash for it, one of the zombies throws a tombstone at him, breaking his leg. The officer sends a call out, which is ignored, and gets ripped apart and devoured by the zombies.

George and Edna soon find their shelter overrun after the zombies use the tombstone as a battering ram and get through the barricade. George, however, finds an oil lamp and throws it at the zombies, setting them on fire. George and Edna get away.

Edna goes to get the police and George resolves himself to destroy the machine the Department of Agriculture was developing, now convinced that it's what is bringing the dead back to life, despite the scientists claiming that it only works on the most primitive nervous systems. He gets to the machine and finds out, to his dismay, that they've managed to boost the range on the machine to five miles.

George smashes the machine and its controls.

The police sergeant is convinced by a colleague that George and Edna are some sort of Satan worshippers. He tells his men to kill them on sight. Edna makes it back to Martin's house, where Martin has been resurrected and he attacks her. She gets away.

George gets Edna to a gas station and heads back to the local morgue with a can of gasoline. He gets caught, however, and the authorities take Martin's body back to the morgue.

As soon as the machine is repaired and switched on, the dead start to rise again. George finds out that Edna is at the hospital and goes to rescue her. He finds her, but the police are hot on his trail and the zombies are on a rampage. Edna gets killed, becomes a zombie, and tries to attack George, but he's already setting the zombies on fire and tosses Edna into the flames. The sergeant shows up and shoots George dead.

Satisfied that he's solved the crimes, the sergeant goes to the Old Owl to sleep for the night. George shows up and attacks him. The sergeant tries to shoot him, to no avail.

The final scenes show the machine back up and running.

Not Very Well Known, but Very Good

Let Sleeping Corpses Lie isn't the most well known of the '70s zombie films, but it's certainly a shade better than some of the more popular ones. The acting is good, the action is staged well, and there's a palpable sense of tension. The story manages to make use of three separate antagonists—the sergeant, the Department of Agriculture workers and their machine, and the risen dead—and does so without the action becoming muddled. As far as horror movies go, this one does a great job of setting up the plot, complicating it with other players, and keeping the entire thing intelligible. There aren't any parts in this film where you'll be wondering what's going on, who a person is, or why they're in the film.

The film also makes great use of scenery, showing off the beauty of the natural environment without letting it overshadow the rest of the action. This film has a sense of place, and the placement of the action is important to how the film unfolds. In this regard, it's up there with the best zombie films, which all tend to use their locations as characters of a sort, whether it's an abandoned farmhouse, a shopping mall, or a remote military outpost outside of London.

To put it in the most basic terms, this movie gives a sense that something is happening, that it's happening in a specific place, and that there's some point to the story other than watching people get slaughtered by zombies.

As stated, the acting in this film is also quite good, particularly for this genre. The police sergeant is a puritanical authoritarian type, who seems convinced that George hates him because George has long hair and a fashionable wardrobe. It's brilliant hypocrisy, in that George is actually quite forthcoming with the police until they start acting like thugs. The sergeant is all judgment and notions of moral superiority, but he doesn't give George and Edna the slightest chance to prove him wrong.

The character remains consistent, as well. He prejudges George, Edna—, and Katie—and that makes him blind to what's going on, even though it should be obvious. He decides what's going on and ignores the facts around him, which are not particularly hard to see. He decides that they're Satanists because that's what he wants to believe. He kills George when the man was clearly trying to stop a massacre and, not only is he smug about it, he wishes he could kill George again. The sergeant is a man driven by arrogance and judgment, not reason, and his position of authority makes him just as much a threat as the zombies menacing the area.

Edna and George area likeable characters. They're both very fashionable, smart and have a chemistry that makes it believable that George would go out of his way to try to save Edna. They bond, and that's apparent in how their characters are portrayed by the actors.

This isn't a great dramatic film but, as far as zombie films go, particularly at this lower budget level, but it's very well done. Edna does the classic slip and fall in front of the zombies, but the clichéd part of that is averted, as she's a fashionable girl wearing heeled boots trying to run on grass and near a river. Of course she'd fall. She's not incompetent, just off-balance. George proves to be crafty and determined to survive, but he doesn't suddenly become a class-A badass out of nowhere. In some ways, he's the good version of what the sergeant so harshly judges him to be. George is a young man with an open mind. He sees what's going on and refuses to let the fact that it goes against what he'd like to believe stop him from acting based on reality.

This is quite a good film all round and, as you're about to see, it's even clever and innovative where the zombies are concerned.

Enjoying These Zombies

These zombies merit some praise. They're slow zombies, of course, and that makes sense, given that this was one of the many films that attempted to cash in on the popularity of zombies as they were portrayed in *Night of the Living Dead*. These zombies, however, are rendered in a very clever and memorable way.

There's a great deal made in this film about how strong the zombies are, which gives them a bit of extra punch, so to speak. They're not fast, but they're fast enough that you can't casually walk away from them as you could zombies in other films. The vagrant zombie seems to have some sort of leadership over the other zombies. He's also shown apparently resurrecting other zombies, even though the machine developed by the scientists is also supposed to be part of that.

The film also makes good use of a limited effects budget in terms of the mad scientist element. The Department of Agriculture personnel are shown out in the field working on their experiments and there's an obvious connection built between the zombies and the machine by the exposition throughout the film. The props for the scientists aren't great by any means, and are even a bit silly, but they work well enough and don't distract. Instead of focusing on the mad scientist's lair, the film focuses on what they're doing, the experimental nature of it, and the fact that they clearly haven't taken into account what might result from their experiments. Like the sergeant, they see what they're predisposed to see, but not much more, unfortunately. That mad-scientist element plays into the zombies, which gives them a nice combination of what appear to be mystical—the vagrant zombie's apparent power—and scientific origins.

These zombies are also clever. They can use tools and, because of their incredible strength, can perform feats such as throwing a gravestone several feet with some degree of accuracy. They band together to break down a barrier and one gets the sense that it's not just their weight that brings down the door. They have some element of will to them, and that makes them frightening.

This film has appropriate gore in it. They show the zombies eating their victims, which is about the most gut-wrenching that it gets. There's a different kind of horror here, however.

This film plays a lot on gothic horror tropes. The atmosphere counts for a lot. The shots of the vagrant zombie wandering around are genuinely creepy. Furthermore, George is a noble hero, Edna a great character to put in danger.

This film is not art cinema, and it's not any sort of a breakthrough in zombie films, storytelling, or special effects. It colors within the lines but also manages to make a good picture in the process. It's worth seeing. Despite the fact that it was made so long ago, it holds up and the dated resources that the police—particular the poor officer that tries to help George and Edna—have, only contributes to the tension. They can't instantly get information or call out for help and, largely, their assumptions are based on silly urban legends rather than solid facts.

The danger in this film doesn't come just from the zombies. It also comes from arrogance, prejudice, and assumptions on the part of the older individuals and, sadly, the young people in this film end up paying the price for that.

This movie is available for rental streaming and is well worth the cost. It's also available on DVD. This is actually an Italian production. The original title is *Non si deve profanare il sonno dei morti*, so you may want to look for it under that name, as well.

Dawn of the Dead (1978)

Director:

George A. Romero

Starring:

David Emge

Ken Foree

Gaylen Ross

Scott Reiniger

This is a sequel to *Night of the Living Dead*, with Romero helming the production. It's arguable whether *Dawn of the Dead* or *Night of the Living Dead* is the most important American zombie film in terms of establishing the genre.

Dawn of the Dead has little in common with the original film plot-wise, though it does include much of the same where the zombies and the situations are concerned. It is incredibly influential, no matter how one looks at it, and is generally regarded as an excellent film by those who love the zombie horror genre.

The Plot

Though it's a sequel to *Night of the Living Dead*, *Dawn of the Dead* doesn't pick up where the other film left off.

The action takes place first in Philadelphia. The crisis has been going on for nearly a month when the movie begins, and it seems like the living are losing ground to the dead. Martial law has been declared. Logically, because they are centers of population, the cities are hit the worst, with the recently dead coming back to life in large numbers. Authorities hard-pressed to beat back the tide of undead.

At an area station, WGON, two of the main characters, Stephen Andres and Francine Parker, want to get out of the city. Andres is a pilot and the two decide to take the traffic chopper to get out of town.

Stephen has a friend who works on the SWAT team, which is engaged in a battle with the zombies and the occupants of a downtown apartment building who are refusing to give their dead up for disposal. After a vicious battle, Roger, Stephen's friend, lets another SWAT team member know about the plot to steal the chopper. Peter, his SWAT compatriot, wants to go, particularly after it becomes apparent that the zombie plague is only getting worse.

The four manage to steal the helicopter and get out of town. They fly aimlessly, almost getting taken out by zombies while refueling the chopper, but manage to find an abandoned shopping mall. They decide to take shelter there, mirroring the action in the first film with the farmhouse.

The shopping mall has plenty of supplies and they steal some nearby semi trucks to block off the entry routes into the building. They find a space and take out what zombies remain in the mall, securing their position.

At first, the situation seems ideal. Because they're in a mall, they have everything they could need, including plenty of food and water to go around. Cabin fever soon sets in, however.

Francine is pregnant, which starts a debate as to whether she should carry the child to term or not. She decides to keep it. Roger gets bitten by a zombie and dies and, of course, he comes back to life, forcing his friend to dispatch him.

Over time, they lose contact with the outside world altogether. At first, there are broadcasts that keep them informed of what's going on, but they eventually stop. They begin to wonder whether

Films of the Dead

civilization has completely fallen apart in the wake of the living dead. Francine learns to fly the helicopter in case something happens to Stephen.

A gang of bikers shows up, raiding the mall and taking what they can. When they break down the barriers that were set up, however, the mall is flooded with zombies and a fight breaks out between the survivors and the bikers. Stephen ends up getting killed by one of the zombies during the fight.

Stephen is resurrected and goes after Francine and Peter. Peter manages to kill Stephen and to get Francine out of the building onto the roof. He follows her, initially thinking of staying behind and making sure that she gets away, but the two end up flying away together in the helicopter.

Similar to the First, but More Developed

This film is both a sequel to and an expansion of *Night of the Living Dead*. The first film had a budget of just over $100,000, putting it firmly into low-budget territory. This one had a budget nearly six times as high, allowing Romero to greatly expand upon the story and the setting.

The higher budget is apparent right from the first action sequence, when we see a running battle through an apartment building between the residents, the authorities, and the living dead. In this film, people are well aware of the living dead and are fighting back actively. There's less of the confusion that we see in the first film.

The theme of isolation really doesn't come into play until sometime after the survivors are trapped in the shopping mall. When the SWAT team members are blocking the entrances with semis, they engage in some very 1970s CB radio chatter, seemingly enjoying themselves.

Things start to get dark in the same way they do in the first film, however. Each day that they are trapped in the mall, tensions increase. As they begin to realize that there may be no civilization to go back to, they become more contentious with one another. The stress wears on them and it takes all that they have to keep themselves together.

The acting in this film is very good, particularly for a horror film, a genre in which the acting is oftentimes lacking. The character development is also good. Roger is a very macho sort of character and, while stealing the semis, he underestimates the zombies and ends up getting bitten, sealing his fate. Peter is more efficient, methodical, and takes the threat more seriously, reminiscent of Ben in the first film.

Francine could have been a liability, given that she's carrying a child, but she ends up being the one who saves herself and the other survivor by learning how to fly the helicopter well enough to get them away from the mall. Stephen, unfortunately, tries to be effective at fighting back the horde, but he's far out of his element if he's not behind the controls of a chopper. He nearly kills Peter at one point, sparking Peter's rage and getting himself a very frightening reminder about the need to know where you're pointing your gun.

All of the characters in this film have strengths and weaknesses, and, at first, they help one another out quite well. Unfortunately, they all share the human weakness—or strength, in a normal situation—of needing to belong to a larger society. As society seems to fade away outside the mall and as they become more isolated, this weakness takes over and they start to fall apart psychologically.

These themes are present in the first film, but the first film takes place on a much smaller scale than this one. In that film, the survivors are trapped in a house with nowhere to go.. Ostensibly, help would be coming in the morning but it doesn't turn out that way.

In this film, there's no apparent end to the wait that the characters have to endure. It doesn't seem like the authorities are making any headway fighting back the zombies, in fact, they seem to be losing ground at a frightening pace. The talking heads on the television only become more contentious as time goes on.

The bikers represent anarchy, of course, riding into the mall and seeming to delight in killing off the zombies. They basically become marauders, adapting to a world where civilization has fully declined and showing that, in the world to come, cohesion is not an option. The strong will survive and, when someone doesn't survive, there's no point in mourning them. It's a hard, cold world that humanity is headed toward, and, given the number of zombies that pour into the mall when the barricades are moved, it seems like humanity is heading there at a frighteningly fast pace.

Where *Night of the Living Dead* was a contained, nihilistic film, this one is much grander in scope, but equally nihilistic. When the two survivors do flee, it's not apparent where they're going to go. Their options seem limited: survive the hordes or survive the bunch of raiders and murderers that society has become.

Interesting Themes

There are some very interesting themes in this film. First, there are some intentionally hilarious scenes where the zombies are wandering around the mall, not looking all that different than a horde of shoppers would look on any given weekend. This is a dig at consumerism, of course, and quite an effective one. Writers have spent a lot of time analyzing this, sometimes to great depth. In fact, this seems to have been taken a bit too far. The obvious reference is enough to make the point. At the time that this film was made, shopping malls were a big part of the culture and symbolic of the mindless consumerism that had replaced the authentic social interactions of days before. In this film, the living dead tear apart the only real cityscape we see. The apartment the police raid is largely populated by people of color, and the officers throw racial epithets around as they make their way through the wreckage. One way to see this is, of course, that society was falling apart due to prejudice, social stratification, and racism before the living dead ever became a problem; the authorities were an expression of this and, in fact, legitimized the use of force that backed that dysfunction.

The film's survivor cast, by way of contrast, includes two white men, a woman and a black man. They all have to stick together to survive, as seen in the first film. In this film, no leader emerges to take the place of Ben, but they all manage to reach a sort of working relationship with one another before things fall apart. They tend to stick to their areas of expertise. Roger and Peter provide the muscle, Stephen has piloting skills, and Francine manages to learn Stephen's skills and replaces him as the pilot following his death.

Traditional authority has also fallen apart in the wake of the zombie apocalypse. The news has guests on who try to explain what's going on, but no one really seems to know why it's happening. After a time, the end of the broadcast signals that civilization, if not completely, has nearly collapsed. Mass communication is a major part of social cohesion, of course, and of disseminating the messages of authority. With the television gone, there's no way for the survivors to know if they're alone or not. The only assurance they get that they're not alone comes in the form of the bikers, who are certainly not who the other survivors want to band together with, though the bikers do seem well-suited to the new world.

In the end, the two smartest survivors are the ones who make it and, given that they're not prone to overestimating themselves in fatal ways, they seem likely to survive for a while. But given that they have nowhere to go, really, it's not apparent what they're flying off into and whether it's even worth surviving at all.

The Gore

There is plenty of gore in this film and it makes quite an impression, even long after the film was made. The gore is a continuation of the major horror theme in the first film: cannibalism.

The *Return of the Living Dead* series launched the association between zombies and eating brains, but in this film, the zombies don't spare much of anything.

In this film, turning into a zombie is inevitable once one dies. No one really knows what causes it, but no one seems to be immune. Some viewers may assume—given the way that Roger dies—that the bite is what causes the transformation. Romero has stated, however, that anyone who dies in his universe will become a zombie. Whatever causes it, it's inevitable. The darkness in this, of course, is that anyone you lose out of your group of friends, you're inevitably going to have to dispatch with a headshot, making the world very bleak.

Enjoying These Zombies

Dawn of the Dead is right next to *Night of the Living Dead* in terms of influence. In *Night of the Living Dead*, the characters were improvising, more than anything. They didn't have much in the way of supplies or weapons and getting out of the house was not an option.

In *Dawn of the Dead*, it seems like the characters are in a much better position, at least at first. They have two experienced fighters with them in the forms of the SWAT team members, who are well armed. They have a pilot and, after Francine learns to fly, they have two, and a helicopter. It shouldn't be too hard for them to get by until the crisis is over, but therein lays the problem—and tension—that drives this story.

Getting out of the city seemed like the logical course of action, but that proved to not improve their situation much at all. The entire world is falling apart and they're just delaying the inevitable by hiding out. Eventually, reality comes crashing through their doors and reminds them that they're out of places to run.

There's a real dilemma here. The characters could run—or fly, as the case may be—but where would they go? Their shopping mall fortress seems like the best place they have to hide out. In the end, it's safe from zombies, but not from humans, who bring the zombies through the door when they launch a raid on the mall.

These zombies are of the slow, shambling sort and that makes them a long-term menace more than a panic-inducing threat. Their numbers keep growing and, while you may be able to outrun them or hide from them for a while, they're going to find you eventually. They don't sleep, they don't run out of breath and they never stop. They're certainty incarnate; as certain as the death that brings them into being.

In *Night of the Living Dead*, the cruelest part of the story occurs when Ben gets gunned down accidentally, mistaken for one of the zombies by the posse that shows up. In *Dawn of the Dead*, the cruelest part of the story is that no posse is going to show up. Help and salvation are a long way away and it's not clear if the final two survivors are going to make it.

This film launched several sequels, some of which are featured in this book. It also firmly established the basic zombie story formula, at least until the fast zombies came about in the early 2000s. Like *Night of the Living Dead*, this film holds up very well.

Debating whether *Night of the Living Dead* or *Dawn of the Dead* is the better film is pointless. Any real fan of zombie films needs to see both. They're very similar in many regards, but *Dawn of the Dead* is much slicker, has a higher budget and is more expansive in its scope. Either one, however, offer plenty of chills and both helped to start off the zombie craze that has yet to end.

Zombi 2 (1979)

Director:

Lucio Fulci

Starring:

Tisa Farrow

Ian McCulloch

Al Cliver

Richard Johnson

Gruesome enough to be banned in several nations, *Zombi 2* was billed as a sequel to *Dawn of the Dead*, but really has no connection to that film. If you're convinced that you can sit through any level of film gore without being revolted, this one should prove a challenge. The film is eerie in the extreme and very atmospheric, as is characteristic of Fulci's work.

The Plot

Zombi 2 starts out in New York, when the police investigate an abandoned yacht. There are clear signs of a struggle and, right from the start, there are some rather repugnant shots of what remains on the yacht. While they're exploring, a zombie attacks the police officers. The zombie is thrown into the harbor, but one of the officers is bitten and killed in the process.

The police trace the boat back to Anne Bowles, whose father was the owner. Her father was a researcher who had sailed off to the Caribbean on a project. She meets up with Peter, a reporter, and they find out that her father had gone to Matool, part of the US Virgin Islands.

They head to the island to find out what happened to her father. They meet Susan and Bryan, who help them to get to Matool.

Bowles's father was investigating a plague on the island. The dead are rising up from their graves to attack the living. Another doctor, Menard, is trying to figure out what's causing the plague. He has a wife named Paola with whom he has conflicts about leaving the island.

One of the most memorable scene in this film occurs shortly after all of this is established. Susan goes scuba diving and runs across a shark. Brian manages to shoot the shark, but it runs into the boat and Susan has to dive to escape.

While she takes shelter in a coral outcropping, a zombie attacks her. She gets away, using the coral itself as a weapon, but the shark and the zombie are soon going at it. The zombie manages to bite the shark, but the shark eventually rips off the zombie's arm and escapes.

Dr. Menard is researching the zombies when he finds out that the zombies are on a rampage all over the island. That night as Paola, Dr. Menard's wife, is taking a shower, she is attacked by a zombie and gets a splinter from a door through her eye.

Shooting the zombies in the head kills them in this film. The zombification process is familiar, with bites passing the zombie curse. The zombies feast on Paola in a particularly gory sequence.

The group is forced to flee the zombies and, as they drive off, they crash their vehicle. They end up in a graveyard, where Peter and Annie find a Spanish-style helmet, such as was worn by the conquistadores, and notice that they are surrounded by gravestones.

A risen conquistador zombie—the one seen on many posters for this film—kills Susan. The zombies continue to rise up as the group flees the scene.

Films of the Dead

Dr. Menard reveals that that Vodou is to blame for the zombies and that he's been trying to end the curse. Fritz ends up attacking the doctor and killing him, and Bryan dispatches him. The zombies begin reanimating all around them and the final showdown plays out, with Peter and Anne taking off with Bryan, who has been bitten. On the boat, they receive a message that the zombies are spreading.

The final shot in the film is of zombies crossing the Brooklyn Bridge.

One of the Best for Gore Fans

If you like your zombie films gory, you'll enjoy *Zombi 2*. Even if you don't care either way about the gore factor, the film still has a lot to offer.

Fulci does a great job of making what could be a tropical paradise into an eerie, remote place. The film captures the element of the unknown that make Vodou zombie films—or at least the good ones—effective.

The film has Romero-style zombies, which means plenty of swarming. The most frantic scenes are built around trying to get shelter from them. The zombies are slow, so it's not hard to get a lead on them, but the characters are also on an island, so there are only so many places to run.

The gore in this film is rather legendary, and while some of the effects may not be on par with modern effects, *Zombi 2* still manages to be revolting. Zombies inflict grievous wounds and, in and of themselves, the zombies are repellent. Many of the goriest scenes are drawn out to heighten the effect.

The Fulci Zombie

The Fulci zombie is disgusting, and brilliantly so. The ones who have been freshly killed look more or less like living people, although usually pallid and covered in blood. They move slowly, gather in large groups, and overwhelm their victims with numbers, or get the best of them with sneak attacks. They seem to be more or less silent, creeping up on characters quite a bit.

The zombies that have been dead for longer—notably the conquistadores—are masterpieces. They're equal parts bone, dirt, slimy remains of flesh, and insects. The conquistador featured on the cover is truly the best in this film, with maggots imbedded in his eye socket.

The zombies rise and move very slowly. The rising-from-the-grave effect in this film is particularly eerie. It does, however, bring up some rather glaring flaws with these zombies

The film has to rely on some pretty silly scenes for the zombies to really pose any sort of a threat. They move incredibly slowly, far slower than the zombies in Romero's film, and seem to be far less intelligent, even compared to the zombies in the first film. These zombies sort of mill around in huge groups and very slowly advance on anything living. It would be easy enough to stay miles ahead of the zombie horde by walking at a normal pace. Many of the zombies seem to have their eyes closed—the older ones sometimes don't appear to have any at all.

When Susan is killed, she just stands there for what seems like forever and screams at the conquistador zombie that kills her. She had more than enough time to run away. and, in fact, she probably could have avoided him just by backing up.

The slow movements of the zombies are most effective in the scenes that show them aimlessly milling around in the dark and in the scenes where they're rising up from the grave.

In terms of being frightening, these zombies are most effective when they sneak up on other characters. The story has to make some unbelievable accommodations to make this happen. Why the doctor didn't just decapitate or headshot all the corpses in the hospital is a mystery, and it ends up being a fatal mistake.

The ending is grim, but also over-the-top enough to be funny. The radio announcer gives a play-by-play of the zombies attacking the radio station and dies with a shrill scream.

The gore levels in this film, however, make it worth tolerating the bizarre behavior of the characters. This film gave us zombie vs. shark, the eyeball splinter, the zombie with the maggots pouring out of its eye, and plenty of other gut-wrenching scenes. It's worth watching just for those.

Enjoying These Zombies

These zombies have a nice origin story in that they stick to the Vodou roots of the legend. They're modern, however, so there are more opportunities for the type of over-the-top gore that this film is known for, and the massive scale of the zombie assault. It's not just a Vodou priest and his mind slaves; it's a horde of zombies risen by a curse rendered large, encompassing the entire island.

All around, the film works and it's worth seeing. It has its shortcomings, but it's widely considered a classic for legitimate reasons, particularly the gore.

The film is available under the titles *Zombie Flesh Eaters* and *Woodoo and Zombie*, as well. There have been several releases by various distributers. The many releases are of varying quality, but there was a version released on Blu-ray by Blue Underground in 2011.

There were also several cuts of this film made, mostly to satisfy censorship schemes overseas. The film, in its complete form, is certainly worthy of a place in any zombie film collection.

Day of the Dead (1985)

Director:

George A. Romero

Starring:

Lori Cardille

Joseph Pilato

Richard Liberty

Terry Alexander

Day of the Dead is the third installment in Romero's zombie films. This one changes the focus a bit. While the two films that preceded this one tended to focus on the crisis created by the dead rising from their graves, this one looks more at the effects the decline of society has had on the living. It also looks at the conflict between those who want to understand what's going on, and those who just want to shoot their way out of a bad situation.

The Plot

This film starts out sometime after the events of *Dawn of the Dead*. At the beginning of the film, the lead character, Dr. Sarah Bowman, is sitting in a plain room staring at a calendar with x's marking off the days. It turns out to be a nightmare and, before she wakes, zombie hands burst through the wall and grab at her.

Since *Dawn of the Dead*, the undead have apparently wiped out civilization for the most part. The first non-dream sequences show Dr. Bowman and her colleagues trying to call out to people on an abandoned Fort Meyers street. The only ones who respond are the undead and they're so numerous at this point that the helicopter pilots can hear the undead wailing over the engines.

They get back to their base, an old missile silo. The small mix of scientists and ex-soldiers seem to have at least some semblance of a community going on, one of them tending a rather lush marijuana grow and another enjoying the sunshine. Below ground, however, things are much tenser.

The soldiers and the scientists have conflict going on between them. Dr. Logan, who the soldiers have nicknamed "Frankenstein", head the scientists. The soldiers and the scientists work together to capture zombies from a system of infested underground tunnels. They deliver them to Frankenstein, who is trying to domesticate them.

The base is very isolated. The radio operator only has World War II-era equipment to work with, so they're unable to contact anyone away from the base. They're also running low on supplies. The leader of the military personnel is Captain Rhodes, an explosive, authoritarian sort whose soldiers are rapidly falling out of line. As Frankenstein puts it at one point: "Your ignorance is exceeded only by your charm, Captain." It's an apt description. The soldiers sexually harass Dr. Bowman and show open contempt for the scientists.

Frankenstein has one zombie that he's been working with named Bub, who seems to show some indication of memory. He salutes the captain when he sees him, indicating that he may have been a military member in life. He also shows a basic knowledge of how to work a firearm, but he's not all there, obviously.

The zombie-gathering missions prove to be dangerous and, soon enough, one of the soldiers gets his throat ripped out by one of the undead. He's mercy-killed by his comrade—Steel—to keep him from coming back as undead, which is inevitable in Romero's films.

Films of the Dead

Dr. Bowman and Pvt. Salazar, one of the soldiers, have been having an affair. This has created tension between Salazar and his fellow soldiers, who also regard him as a coward. A zombie bites Salazar, forcing Bowman to amputate the arm so he doesn't become infected.

Unfortunately, people who are apparently losing their minds surround Dr. Bowman and everyone else who's remotely sane. The captain is becoming increasingly violent, and Frankenstein has been using dead soldiers to feed the zombies.

Bowman, Salazar, the pilot and the communications expert decide to take off before things get worse, but the captain and his men find out what Frankenstein is up to and gun him down.

The captain takes Dr. Bowman her colleagues, gunning down one of them when the pilot, John, refuses to take the captain and his men in his helicopter.

The captain then threatens to throw Dr. Bowman and McDermott, John's copilot, to the zombies. John attempts to stop them, but gets thrashed by Steel. They manage to escape, however.

The captain and his men realize that Salazar has sabotaged the controls for the base. Salazar not only allows the zombies through the fence protecting the base, he allows them to eat him and lowers the elevator that seals off the silo once they're all in the base, flooding it with zombies.

The zombie Frankenstein was so proud of, Bub, breaks free. He finds the doctor and, seeming to recall his humanity, shows emotion and seeks revenge for the slaying of the doctor.

Bub actually shows quite a bit of development. He goes after Steel but, rather than trying to rip him apart and devour him, he actually takes a shot at Steel. The zombie is clearly capable of relearning the skills he had in life.

Steel manages to get away from Bub, but he gets cornered by the zombies in Frankenstein's lab and shoots himself to avoid being eaten alive. Bub does manage to put a couple of rounds in the captain, however, gunning him down in the hallway and getting revenge for Frankenstein. The captain is eventually eaten after Bub manages to put another round in him, salute him, and leave him to his fate. He dies a particularly gruesome death, even for a Romero film.

John, McDermott, and Bowman make it back to the chopper and fly off to an island, as John had suggested doing at the beginning of the film. Bowman still has nightmares, understandably, and continues crossing days off a calendar.

An Interesting Twist

In Romero's first two films, the action comes from the survivors trying to battle back the zombies. There are shades of personal and social breakdown in both, but these aspects are more in focus in *Day of the Dead*.

Though it's not developed much in the plot, Dr. Bowman is working on a way to reverse the zombification process. Frankenstein believes that he can domesticate the zombies and, at least judging by his work with Bub, he seems to be correct. Bub shows an increasing level of intelligence, culminating in not only his anger over the death of Frankenstein, but also figuring out how to use a gun and holding a grudge against the men responsible.

In this regard, Romero's zombies start to show signs that they're evolving. They may not be doing so among themselves but, exposed to a system of basic rewards for good behavior, they seem to catch on.

The zombies also seem to remember who they were before they rose and carry with them the skills they learned in their former lives. This is an interesting twist on the zombie, as most of them are portrayed as being utterly mindless.

The real monsters in this film, in fact, are human beings. The soldiers become increasingly violent and hostile toward the scientists. Eventually, they decide to abandon their mission and to leave the scientists behind, though their plans are foiled when the base is overrun with living dead.

Frankenstein also shows some gruesome personality flaws. He conducts exceptionally morbid experiments, at one point having dissected a zombie so that only his brain and brain stem were visible above the neck. He seems enchanted with what he finds when doing so, even though his other research is indicating that these zombies, in fact, do have some humanity left in them.

Bowman and her two compatriots seem to be the only real human beings left in the mix. Salazar may have been at one time, but he's gone so far into hopelessness that he ends up being a liability to all of them and is the cause of the base being completely overrun with undead.

John is also interesting in that, at the beginning of the film, he comes up with the only plan that really makes any sense in the scenario. He suggests that they just leave and fly away to some island somewhere.

That makes perfect sense, given that they can't communicate with anyone who would be in charge of their mission, and that there doesn't really seem to be any survivor presence. For all they can tell, they're among the last people left on Earth, so what they intend to do if they succeed in their mission really isn't clear. If Bowman managed to reverse the zombification process, they'd still have to distribute the cure she came up with and it's not clear how they'd do that. If Frankenstein succeeded in domesticating zombies, he'd have billions of them, presumably, to domesticate, making his work almost pointless.

Leaving is the only thing that makes sense here. As is the case in *Dawn of the Dead*, the protagonists end up fleeing, but they're fleeing humanity as well as fleeing the zombies. Oddly enough, Bub the zombie shows some element of loyalty when he avenges

Frankenstein. He, undead that he is, shows more humanity than some of the soldiers at the base show.

Enjoying These Zombies

Romero's trademark gore is on full display here, so the fact that the zombies aren't the only threat doesn't means that the audience doesn't get to see plenty of cannibalism.. The movie, in fact, has plenty of rather revolting moments, as should any good zombie film.

The soldiers in this film are a bit over the top. Their acting is a bit much at times and, for the most part, they're menacing in the way a bunch of drunken partiers would be menacing. They seem wild and out of control, and in some regards, it's hard to imagine how these guys would have ever really cut it in the military, anyway. They don't give off any real indication of being efficient, or working well together, so they come off more as a gang of armed and dangerous idiots than soldiers.

The film, however, does do well in terms of setting up a situation that is rather nightmarish. The experiments that go on at the military base are gruesome and heartless and it almost makes the viewer feel bad for the zombies. They go from being sources of terror to somewhat sympathetic characters. When Bub starts to show signs that he remembers who he is or, at least, what hedoes, it becomes even more ambiguous as to who the bad guys and who the good guys are.

Bub manages to aim and fire a handgun, which shows that he possesses more intelligence than most animals, so there's definitely something left of a human being in him. This makes one wonder if the zombies in these films, underneath it all, are caught in some horrible nightmare where they can somewhat remember who and what they were but are driven to eat human flesh and are rotting and falling apart before their own eyes.

Films of the Dead

This film also has an ambiguous role for the solider characters. One would think that being in a military base with a group of armed and trained killers would be the best possible situation in the zombie apocalypse. This film, however, explores the idea that you can't just hole up forever and expect everything to stay cohesive. The crew in *Dawn of the Dead* started to fall apart after some time in the mall, but not like this. They were unprepared to deal with what was going on and that drove the tension. In *Day of the Dead*, the characters are very adept at handling the zombies, even capturing them as needed, but just have no point in going on, really, and that starts tearing them apart.

Romero would build on his universe in later films. This film gets good ratings from critics and despite its weaknesses manages to get the point across. It's unlike the first two films in the series, centering more on human versus human than human versus zombie.. This film offers something more than that.

Probably the most interesting thing about this film is that it poses the following question: When is it time to just give up and accept that civilization has fallen? John really seems to have the right idea here. Eventually, when there are far more dead than living in the world, heading off to a tropical island and enjoying life is about all one can do.

Re-Animator (1985)

Director:

Stuart Gordon

Starring:

Jeffrey Combs

Bruce Abbott

Barbara Crampton

Oftentimes billed as *H.P. Lovecraft's Re-Animator*, this film follows a mad scientist, his unwitting roommate-cum-partner and the people unfortunate enough to be involved in their lives as they further Herbert West's research into resurrecting the dead. This film has plenty of gore and one of the most gut-wrenching—and morbidly amusing—climaxes you'll find anywhere.

The Plot

When we first meet Herbert West, the titular re-animator, he's bringing a dead professor at the University of Zurich back to life. He's interrupted by the faculty and authorities just as the professor comes back to life and the professor dies a horrific death—his second one, apparently—due to West using too much of his glowing, green reagent to resurrect him.

The action shifts to Miskatonic University, a fictional university that figures prominently into Lovecraft's mythos.

West is a brilliant student and gets a room with Dan Cain, who is also studying for his MD at the university. He immediately asserts his own arrogance by questioning the skills of Dr. Hill, one of the professors at Miskatonic, and a respected researcher. He accuses the doctor of stealing his work from another researcher.

West moves into Cain's house and, soon after, things get bizarre. Cain's cat, Rufus, disappears and he and his girlfriend, Megan, go looking for him. Megan is horrified to find Rufus in West's refrigerator. Confronted about this, West says that the cat got its head stuck in a jar and suffocated. He noticeably uses the word "it" to describe the cat, while Cain and Megan refer to Rufus as a "he," hinting that West doesn't see animals—or humans—as anything but things to experiment on. It's readily apparent that, despite his brilliance, West is a complete psychopath and narcissistic in the extreme.

Later that night, Cain is awakened by the sound of yowling from the basement. He goes downstairs to find West being attacked by a resurrected Rufus. Cain manages to subdue and re-kill the cat. He doesn't believe West when West says he brought the cat back to life, but West re-animates the cat a second time with his reagent. Megan comes down into the basement and is overwhelmed with disgust at the poor cat's fate—it's nearly torn in half when they bring it back to life. Her dislike of West grows.

Dr. Hill has a driving hatred of West as well. He's also got an obsession with Megan and is jealous of Cain. Megan's father, Dr. Halsey, is the Dean of Miskatonic, and Hill works hard to set up a conflict between Halsey, Cain and West. He eventually gets Cain and West thrown out of the school.

West and Cain, however, conspire a way to get into the morgue so that they can test out West's work on dead human beings. West manages to re-animate a corpse but, like Rufus, it immediately becomes aggressive. During a melee with the corpse, it knocks down the door of the morgue, crushing Dr. Halsey, who is outside screaming to be let in. West drives a bone saw through the corpse's chest, killing it again. He then reanimates Dr. Halsey, but he's a shadow of his former self.

Halsey is given over to the care of Dr. Hill, who gives him a lobotomy with his invention, a laser drill. Cain and Megan find files in Hill's cabinets that detail his creepy obsession with Megan.

Hill, meanwhile, goes after West. He shows up in West's basement laboratory, and is more than impressed with West's work. He threatens to take credit for it. West kills Hill with a shovel, severing Hill's head from his body in the process.

Realizing that he's never really reanimated whole parts before, West puts Hill's head in a pan and re-animates it. Hill isn't as zombified as Halsey and, in fact, retains control over his body. His body attacks West, knocks him unconscious, and steals all of West's work.

Hill is apparently resurrected with a great deal of power, and he manages to control Halsey. He gets Halsey after he gets Megan and Cain. He then disguises himself by putting a model head on his body and having his body put his head in a bag. He heads to the morgue, easily getting by the security guard, who goes on break.

Halsey kidnaps Megan and brings her to the morgue, where Hill begins tormenting her. He has learned that, with his new laser drill, he can lobotomize people in a way that gives him complete control over them. Cain and West show up and Cain frees Megan. West confronts Hill and, with enough of his consciousness left for him to remember her, Halsey is persuaded to help the trio when Megan reaches out to him.

Hill, however, says that he has a plan and several corpses rise up from the tables. Halsey helps by fighting them off Megan and Cain. Halsey goes after Hill and destroys his severed head. West says he has a theory, yells "Overdose!" and injects Hill's body with enough reagent to kill him, or so West believes.

After being injected with a huge amount of the reagent, Hill's torso opens up and his intestines lash out, grabbing West. Knowing he's doomed, West screams for Cain to save his research. Cain and Megan flee.

The zombies, however, are still on a rampage and go after the pair. One of them attacks Megan in an elevator. Cain grabs a fire axe and cuts off its hand, then sticks his finger in its brain through a horrific wound on the side of its head, incapacitating the corpse.

Megan has had her throat crushed by the zombie, however. Cain tries to bring her back, mirroring a scene at the beginning of the film where a nurse advises him that a good doctor knows when to give up. The staff in the emergency room leave and Cain takes West's reagent and injects it into Megan. The screen fades, with the glowing reagent fading out last, and Megan screams as the movie ends.

Really Gory

This film is exceptionally gory. It's so over-the-top about it, however, that it comes off as comical quite a bit of the time, though it still is enough to nauseate even strong-stomached individuals.

The re-animated corpses tend to bleed out of their mouths almost constantly. They all have horrific wounds. Dr. Hill's severed head manages to speak in a menacing, grating tone, even though there aren't any lungs attached to push air through his throat and mouth.

There are some supernatural implications to the reagent in how Hill is able to control his body, despite his spine being severed. The lobotomy procedure he does using the electric drill also puts the victims under his mind control, making Dr. Hill something of a mad scientist combined with a Vodou practitioner.

The film is gruesome all around, starting with the professor's reaction to too much reagent in Zurich, proceeding through to peeling the skin off of someone's skull, and getting even more gory from there on out. If you love gore, this film will be a lot of fun. If you don't, you're probably going to be horrified by what takes place on the screen, or just have a good time being a bit grossed out.

The Mad Scientist and His Zombies

Herbert West is every bit the mad scientist in this film. He seems to have little or no capacity for relating to other human beings. He believes that every doctor's ultimate goal is to defeat death, and, since he's done as much, that makes him the ultimate doctor, it seems.

Of course, West doesn't seem to care much for making people comfortable or curing disease. When one of West's reanimated corpses kills Dr. Halsey, his immediate reaction is to be elated that he has a very fresh corpse to work, with rather than showing any sort of remorse over Halsey's death.

He does seem to have something of a friendship with Cain, but only because it serves his purposes. His only other significant interactions with other human beings in the film is his rivalry with Dr. Hill. Hill, essentially, is a dumbed-down, older version of West, but with all of West's arrogance and psychopathy. When Hill discovers what West is up to, his reaction is not revulsion at the immoral and horrific nature of it all, but a desire to claim credit for himself. Like West, he seems to have a god complex that puts all other god complexes to shame.

The zombies in this film are about as gruesome as they come, but they don't really drive the plot. Even when Hill is resurrected, it's implied that his actions are just a continuation of the evil that was already inside of him. He's free to do whatever he wants after being killed by West, essentially freeing him from the threat of being held responsible for his actions, given that he's already a dead man, and a decapitated one at that.

Cain is a good-guy character, but one who is easily drawn into West's plans. One gets the idea that Cain's weakness is that he wants to save everyone, and, of course, considering that West managed to figure out how to bring back the dead, this has obvious appeal to Cain.

The Lovecraft Connection

There are many films out there that invoke H.P Lovecraft's name but have little to do with his stories. *Re-Animator* is among them. H.P Lovecraft was a writer of weird fiction and cosmic horror who was published many times in the pulp magazine *Weird Tales*. While this film has the words "H.P. Lovecraft's..." before the title, it really has nothing to do with the story *Herbert West—Reanimator*, upon which it is ostensibly based.

This particular story appeared in the magazine *Home Brew* and deviated significantly from Lovecraft's usual style of writing. It is very similar to Mary Shelley's *Frankenstein*. In the story, West conducts a series of experiments over many years to reanimate the dead. He eventually ends up working as a medic during World War I, where he has a limitless supply of bodies and parts to work with. The corpses he reanimates seem to relive the moments before their deaths.

Eventually, West moves back to New England and continues his experiments. Later, the resurrected dead exact a horrible vengeance upon him, disemboweling him. The narrator in the story is driven mad by what he sees, and is regarded as insane by the police, to whom he relates at least parts of the story.

Herbert West—Reanimator is widely considered to be one of Lovecraft's worst stories. Some of the elements of the story are mirrored in the film *Re-Animator*, however. Namely, one of the corpses in the story replaces his own missing head with a wax head, in much the same way that Hill replaces his own missing head with a medical model head. The corpses do get their revenge on West in the end, as well. Halsey and some of the other names appear in both stories, and there is the implication that West is a driven man who sees only his goals and not the awful consequences that they invoke.

Enjoying These Zombies

People who love gore fests will love this film. It's campy in the extreme when the blood really starts flying, but it still manages to be gut-wrenching at times.

This film is quite different to many other films involving the resurrected dead in that it crosses the line between mad scientist, Vodou mind control, and a traditional zombie film. The mad scientist element is obvious enough, but when Hill starts controlling the other resurrected dead with his mind, it's very reminiscent of films such as *White Zombie*, where someone uses seemingly supernatural powers to get the dead to do their bidding. It also has elements of a traditional zombie film, particularly during the rampage at the end where the zombies mindlessly try to kill anything that breathes.

This film also features Barbara Crampton, who is one of the most popular scream queens of the 20th century. She appeared in *From Beyond*, another film that was billed as a Lovecraft adaptation but that was a bit closer to meeting that goal than this one.

Whether or not this film ratesas a Lovecraft adaptation is irrelevant to enjoying it. It has many of the elements that made the mad scientist films of the '50s and '60s, and is fun to watch, with the gore very much updated, of course. It also has a lot of elements of *Frankenstein* to it, though it foregoes the gothic trappings and is rooted firmly in the world of today's science. The reagent is far less dramatic than Dr. Frankenstein's elaborate electrical contraption, as featured in the James Whale version of that story, of course, but is actually a bit closer to Shelley's portrayal, where the means of resurrecting the dead is only discussed in the most fleeting ways. In this film, we just trust that the glowing green liquid can really bring back the dead, and to demonstrate it, the film gives us plenty of angry, homicidal corpses to deal with.

This film also follows the typical zombie convention in that the reanimated corpses seem to be homicidal as soon as they get up from their slabs. There is a moment where West believes that one of the corpses—Halsey—shows some awareness of who he is. It's not fully realized until the resurrection of Hill and at the end of the film, where Megan manages to get to her father by reminding him who she is and resurrecting some of his consciousness to go along with his body. Other than that, the zombies are essentially relentless killing machines, as in other films.

This film is a must-see for anyone who likes mad scientist films. It's also great for its rather low-budget trappings. Most of the action takes place on a few sets and the special effects work, but are clearly special effects, nonetheless. There really aren't any parts of this film where something looks so real that it makes you jump out of your seat, but it's gory enough, to be sure.

This film spawned sequels and has a cult following. Its divergence from the Lovecraft story it claims to be based on isn't necessarily a bad thing, since *Herbert West—Reanimator* is considered to be a weak example of his style. Overall, this film has plenty of gore, plenty of zombies and plenty of horror, and should keep just about anyone happy if they're looking for those things in a film.

Like many other zombie films, this film's weaknesses sometimes translate to strengths The over-the-top special effects and psychopathy of the title character just make it more fun to watch, rather than detracting from it.

Return of the Living Dead (1985)

Director:

Dan O'Bannon

Starring:

James Karen

Clu Gulager

Don Calfa

Return of the Living Dead is based on a novel with the same name, but it bears little resemblance to it in its finished form. Written by John A. Russo, who worked with George Romero on *Night of the Living Dead*, this film represents where Russo, primarily used zombie mythology. It's a zom com, and one that's responsible for some of the most trademark elements of the zombie genre..

The Plot

The main character, Freddy, has just gotten a job at a medical supply warehouse. His training involves being shown how to fill an order for a skeleton. His supervisor, Frank, decides to show him some of the more gruesome things to be found in the warehouse.

After looking at bisected dogs and other horrors, Frank takes Freddy down to the basement. In the basement are some barrels that were sent to the warehouse by mistake. They contain bodies, which were sealed up following a government experiment went awry.

Frank slaps one of the barrels to assure Freddy that it's safe, causing it to leak gas. They're both exposed and when the gas dissipates they check the barrel. The body that was in the barrel is gone.

Frank explains that the government was developing a chemical agent when it was found that it resurrected the dead. They sealed the bodies in the barrels to keep the problem contained. This leaked out, however, and was the inspiration for the movie *Night of the Living Dead*. The government forced the filmmakers to change key elements of the film, however, to keep the truth from getting out.

The gas that leaked out of the barrel starts to resurrect the bodies—and the bisected animals—in the warehouse. Frank calls the owner of the warehouse, Burt, and lets him know what happened. They try to kill off one of the resurrected dead, but cannot. Burt asks the mortician across the road, whom he's known for many years, to help him dispose of the body by incinerating it. The mortician, Ernie, agrees.

Freddy has some friends who want to pick him up after work. They party in a graveyard while they're waiting for Freddy's shift to end. While they're partying, the smoke from the crematorium where Burt and Ernie are incinerating the zombie mixes with the rain and falls down onto the cemetery. The dead start to rise and go after the living.

Freddy's girlfriend goes to look for Freddy and heads to the supply warehouse. The zombie from the barrel, who escaped after the barrel broke apart, attacks her.

Everyone is soon on the run as the zombies go on a rampage. Ernie calls in the paramedics for Freddy and Frank after they start to fall ill from their exposure to the gas. The paramedics show up and figure out that Freddy and Frank are both dead already.

Freddy's friends make it to the mortuary and everyone tries to barricade themselves in. The zombies attack, killing the paramedics and the police officer that are called in to assist.

Freddy and Frank are locked away, along with Freddy's girlfriend, who doesn't want to leave him. The zombies in this film are somewhat intelligent, talking on the radio and forming groups to

Films of the Dead

attack with some degree of organization. The survivors interrogate one of the zombies— or its torso, at least. It tells them that they seek out brains to kill the pain of being dead.

The group tries to escape, but all end up trapped in the warehouse together. The survivors call the emergency number printed on the side of the military barrels, but the number belongs to the man in charge of the operation.

The army responds by nuking the area, killing everyone, alive and undead. Unfortunately, this causes the toxin to be distributed via rain once more, and the film ends implying that the contamination is spreading.

Braaaains!

This movie, for the most part, brought the association with zombies eating brains into popular culture. However, the mood in this film is far different than it is in Romero's development of the living dead concept.

Return of the Living Dead, is a comedy. It's technically dark humor, given the undead presence, the violence, and the gore, but it's also very spontaneous and relies on a lot of slapstick and cheesy dialogue. This isn't subtle dark comedy, in essence.

The zombies in this film exhibit some considerable intelligence compared to how they behave in Romero's films. For instance, they not talk, but carry on conversations and answer questions. They also understand how certain actions get certain results. The zombie at the ambulance, for example, requests that the dispatcher send more paramedics, because he wants more paramedics to eat, and the zombie from the barrel uses tools to try to break through the door where Freddy's girlfriend is hiding.

This isn't one of the films where it takes some times before a corpse stands up and starts attacking. The dead rise very quickly. It's a comedy, so there's no need to use the zombies to invoke horror, but they do need to be there for most of the jokes to work.

Enjoying These Zombies

This film is very 1980s and, as anyone who loves film knows, comedy tends not to hold up well over time. Whether or not this film works depends upon one's sense of humor and whether they want to watch a zombie movie that's actually frightening or not. This movie is not scary. The zombie that comes out of the barrel is, by far, the most frightening one of all, but the fear is more based on his appearance than anything else.

With characters with name combinations like Burt and Ernie, it's obvious that the writers were not going for serious chills. There are, however, some fine special effects on display here and, even so long after the film was released, they're still pretty gut-wrenching at times. The gore is done very well and, in some cases, the zombie makeup effects are still impressive. They're not as realistic as the effects that you'll see in modern films, but they're good.

Some of the jokes will seem very dated. Freddy's friends are, essentially, cartoon punk rockers. There's some nudity in the film, and it's definitely intended for an older audience, but the humor in it makes it obvious that it was also intended for teenagers.

This film is important to zombie films in general in that it does firmly establish the "Brains!" trope. As zombie films in generally go, Romero's work seems to have held up much better than this, and, as zombie comedies got more sophisticated and darker—*Zombieland*, for instance—they got better. However, It's still worth watching *Return of the Living Dead*.

The Serpent and the Rainbow (1988)

Director:

Wes Craven

Starring:

Bill Pullman

Zakes Mokae

Cathy Tyson

Paul Winfield

While zombie films have moved gradually away from the Vodou origins of the mythology, *The Serpent and the Rainbow* goes right back to those roots. In this film, a pharmaceutical company wants to research zombification as a possible lead toward a breakthrough anesthetic. Dennis Alan finds out that there is much more to the process than can be explained by a drug.

The Plot

The film introduces the main character, Dennis Alan, as he's talking with natives in the Amazon, after having gotten a new drug for the pharmaceutical company that employs him. He drinks a potion made by a mystic of the tribe and has an intense vision in which he first appears to be attacked by, but then embraces, a jaguar. Arms jutting out of the soil then attack him.

The pharmaceutical company wants him to head to Haiti next. They're interested in the zombification drug used by Vodou practitioners and believe that it could lead to a breakthrough in anesthesia drugs.

Dennis heads to Haiti and works with a doctor named Marielle. He quickly runs afoul of the Tonton Macoute, and a campaign of intimidation begins. At the same time, he investigates the zombification process by tracking down an old man who claimed to have been made into a zombie, and by contacting local Vodou practitioners to obtain the powder.

Eventually, he gets arrested by the Tonton Macoute and is tortured at the hands of Peytraud, a captain—and a brutal one at that. He finds out that the zombie powder he had been given was not the real thing, but manages to track down the practitioner once more and sets up a deal to get the actual zombification powder. While this is going on, Peytraud seems to have gained some access to Dennis through mystical means, invading his dreams. The Tonton Macoute sets him up as a murderer and ejects him from the nation.

While he's getting ready to take off on the plane, the Vodou practitioner who had been dealing with Dennis shows up and gives him a vial of the real powder. Dennis promises him that he's going to be famous for the good the drug will do.

Dennis is safe at home, but Peytraud's power is such that he can reach out to torment Dennis, even in Boston. While Dennis is having a dinner, one of the women at the table is possessed by the captain.

Dennis believes he has to return to Haiti to deal with Peytraud. He ends up being buried alive, but is dug out by the same Vodou priest who gave him the powder. He goes after the captain, knowing that he has Marielle in custody.

The captain and Dennis have their final showdown in the torture room where Dennis was tormented. After nearly losing to the captain, the Jaguar spirit that Dennis encountered in his Amazon vision helps him and Captain Peytraud is dragged into the ground in his own torture chair. Marielle and Dennis both survive.

Very Eerie

This film is definitely worth watching. It strays from the book in being more mystical, but, as a horror film, it works. There are two main threats in this film, which turn out to be very closely linked.

The Tonton Macoute is the primary, and very believable, threat. They're brutal, operate according to their own rules, and the populace is terrified of them. Dennis makes the mistake of drawing their attention and, during the scenes where they are torturing Dennis, it's apparent why people are so afraid of this group.

The second threat in the film is, of course, the Captain Peytraud's Vodou power, which serves to tie together the mystic threat and real threat of the Tonton Macoute all in one. As was mentioned in a previous chapter, the Tonton Macoute was associated with Vodou, and it works to frightening effect here.

This film is more about mind control than being attacked by zombies. In fact, being killed by a zombie isn't really the threat here. The threat is that you could end up as one.

The implication that Peytraud's power is so great that he can reach from Haiti all the way to Boston to possess someone is also frightening. This film is effective in not making Vodou something to laugh at or a primitive religion that needs a scientist to plumb its secrets and find out that it's all totally explainable. In this film, Vodou is, indeed, terrifying.

Vodou in this film represents political power and depends on a knowledge of both the type of chemicals that Dennis is after and something far more powerful than that. The film makes great use of both. The film's worst case scenarios are being poisoned by the zombie drug, being buried alive while fully alert, and being under the control of a Vodou master. It's not an original idea, but it's scary enough. Giving the zombie powder a hint of the scientific by explaining what it's made of and how it works adds to the effect.

The ending sequences go over the top with the magical themes, but they're effective. If the mystical elements of this film don't work for you, the brutality and power of the Tonton Macoute certainly should pack enough punch to make it memorable.

Enjoying These Zombies

This isn't a zombie film that gives you anything in the way of apocalyptic action sequences or invasions by hordes of the undead. The undeath in this film is far more frightening than it is most of these films, and that's notable.

The Serpent and the Rainbow didn't really catch on in the way that many of Craven's films did, and it certainly didn't spawn any sequels. Critics generally didn't like it, but some critics, including Roger Ebert, praised the film as being quite good.

As Ebert and others have pointed out, this film doesn't make a joke out of Vodou. The Haitians are not presented as uneducated and naïve primitives who are afraid of silly supernatural beliefs. There's very good reason to be afraid of the more twisted Vodou practitioners in this film and of the knowledge they have.

This film also manages to show both good people and bad people who are involved in Vodou. It doesn't cast the religion as inherently evil and that serves the story well. Haiti is presented as brutal, but, at the time this story takes place, it most certainly was. The Haitian people shown are intelligent, sympathetic and knowledgeable. This film gets ugly, but not in the ways that films about Vodou have in the past, such as in *King of the Zombies*.

This is a worthwhile film, particularly if one gets bored with the modern zombies. It does an excellent job of showing why the Vodou zombie is a great legend and how it really can be as frightening, and even more frightening, than the best modern zombie films.

It's worth mentioning that Pullman is also great in this film. His character comes off as someone who has respect for the cultures he encounters and manages to obtain to some of their closely guarded secrets, as well, which makes him entirely likeable.

Dead Alive, AKA Braindead (1992)

Director:

Peter Jackson

Starring:

Timothy Balme

Diana Penalver

Elizabeth Moody

Ian Watkin

Dead Alive is the North American release title of the 1992 Peter Jackson film *Braindead*. This same Peter Jackson brought us *The Lord of the Rings* trilogy and *The Hobbit* movies. It's quite a different film from those, demonstrating Jackson's abilities as a gore director and his love of Romero's films. For those who like the gore turned up to 11, this film is right up there with Fulci's, but is much lighter and funnier in addition.

The Plot

Dead Alive starts out by giving us a great back-story for the zombie virus. The Sumatran rat-monkeys spread the zombie virus. These monkeys came about after infected rats raped tree monkeys.

The protagonist is Stewart, who has managed to capture one of these monkeys for himself. The natives don't want him to take it and make a pretty frightening display to convey that fact, but he manages to abscond with the monkey and get away.

Unfortunately, the monkey bites Stewart, prompting his cohorts to cut off his hand. Finding that he's been attacked all over his body, the crew amputates his other arm and then just decides to kill him.

The monkey makes it back to New Zealand, where we're introduced to the main characters in the film. Lionel is a nice guy, but his mother, Vera, is a bit clingy, almost to the levels that Norman Bates had to put up with. Paquita is Lionel's love interest for the film and she's very much into him.

It's not long before the rat-monkey causes more mayhem. Lionel takes Paquita to the zoo but, of course, mother can't have him enjoying himself, so she follows along. The monkey bites her, setting this film's zombie plague in motion.

Vera starts to develop what looks like an outrageously disgusting infection where she was bitten. She begins to literally fall apart, and Lionel has to glue parts of her skin back in place. She also starts to manifest the typical zombie appetite for living flesh, this time starting with a dog.

Vera becomes patient zero, spreading the zombie plague. Lionel does a good job of trying to hide it, but it gets worse and worse as more people are infected. He tries to sedate his mother, but to very little use.

Vera finally appears to die when she is hit in a traffic accident but, of course, she's not dead. Lionel manages to pull off her funeral and, after she's buried, goes to the graveyard to retrieve her. A group of thugs, however, interrupts him and Vera goes on the attack.

Les, one of the non-zombie antagonists in this film, starts bullying Lionel about his inheritance. Les, in the meantime, has decided to have a party at the house. Lionel decides to kill off the zombies by poisoning them, but the poison is a stimulant that sends them into a killing spree.

The action involves everything up to and including a zombified baby, which jumps with surprising speed. The guests mostly get eaten; Paquita manages to survive the attack, but ends up running throughout the house, eventually hiding in the kitchen until the zombie baby and others attack.

In the meantime, Vera has mutated and become huge. Lionel comes back into the house with a lawnmower strapped to his chest and begins attacking the zombies with it, leading to the perhaps the most famous scene in the movie, and certainly one of the goriest.

The house is soon soaked in blood and guts and it appears, for a moment, that the worst has passed. Then Vera appears. She chases Paquita and Lionel out onto the roof. There's a moment where Lionel reveals that he knows that his mother murdered his father, who was having an affair, and that he isn't afraid of her anymore. In response, the zombified Vera opens up her womb and pulls Lionel in, saying that no one will ever love him like her.

Lionel cuts his way out of the womb and Vera falls into the burning house, which caught fire during the chaos of the final zombie slaughter.

The film ends with Lionel and Paquita covered in blood, but otherwise okay, walking away from the burning house just as the firefighters arrive.

Beyond Gory

The plot of this film is basic for a zombie film—someone is bitten, bites others, and the plague spreads. What makes it the cult classic is, quite simply, the insane level of gore.

The camera seems to be in love with anything disgusting that Jackson puts up on screen. The zombies are typically covered in slime, there's plenty of filth, and, when they're otherwise defeated, zombies can even use their intestines and other organs to attack.

As the film progresses, the gore becomes more and mover over-the-top. The final sequence, with the lawnmower, is legendary. Blood flies out of the device in sheets and the zombies are hacked to pieces, with arms, legs, and half-heads sliding around the room.

Selwyn, the baby, is also a nice touch. His parents became zombies before he was born, giving some motivation to have a zombie baby in the film. There are some hilarious scenes of Lionel and the baby at a park, and, generally, whenever the baby shows up on the screen, it's a good sign that something odd and disgusting is about to happen.

If gore isn't your thing, you're not going to enjoy *Dead Alive*. If you're a gore hound, you really can't do better than this film. This film turns the gore up to 11 and beyond. It's so over the top that it's hilarious after a while, and really, that seems to be the point.

There isn't a lot that's innovative here as far as the plot goes. It's a conventional zombie film wrapped in a love story between Lionel and Paquita. It's what Jackson does with it visually that makes it so memorable.

Enjoying These Zombies

These zombies are for those who love gore and for those people alone. They mutate a bit, are generally slathered in something shiny and disgusting-looking, and fall apart almost constantly. They spread the plague by biting, so there's plenty of motivation for them to attack anyone and everyone who crosses their path.

The zombies in this film are surprisingly fragile, leading to some of the best gore scenes, such as Lionel gluing his mother's skin back on. There are some shades of other films in this one as well, particularly *Psycho*, in how the dominated Lionel hides his mother's rotting body away. Of course, in this film, the mother really is the killer and the mood is far lighter than it is in the Hitchcock classic.

Films of the Dead ■ 173

The entire point of these zombies is to be massacred, and that's what the end of the film delivers on, big time. They are similar to Romero's zombies in that they can function after having their limbs amputated, and in that their heads seem to continue living if they're removed from the body. One poor, living, half-a-head gets kicked back and forth during the film's climactic melee. Their innards are also animate. The film really goes far beyond the headshot trope and shows Lionel and the others killing zombies however they can. The real danger with these zombies, however, is that their amputated limbs can continue attacking.

These zombies are, more than anything, silly and fun. The point of this movie is to gross the audience out, and it's still known as being one of the goriest films ever made. It didn't fare terribly well when it was released, but has become more popular as Jackson's reputation as a serious film director grew over the years. This is a must-see for any fan of Jackson or zombies, and certainly film lovers who enjoy gore.

There are some Easter eggs in here that fans of Jackson may want to check out. For instance, the scenes on Skull Island take place in the same location where parts of *The Lord of the Rings* were filmed. Skull Island, where the Sumatran Rat-Monkey comes from, gets its name from *King Kong*, and is revisited by the director again when he did the remake of that film in 2005. The island is fictional, of course, but it's a great setting for exotic action and frightening creatures and natives.

If you want a bloody good time with zombies, check out *Dead Alive*.

The Dead Hate the Living! (2000)

Director:

Dave Parker

Starring:

Eric Clawson

Jamie Donahue

Brett Beardslee

The Dead Hate the Living! Is a low-budget zombie film from Full Moon Entertainment, a company with a reputation for releasing low-budget horror fare. This is among the films featuring zombies that came out before the current craze started, and it portrays the creatures in ways quite different from *28 Days Later*

The Plot

This film has a very barebones plot, but goes into a great deal of exposition at times. Essentially, a group of independent filmmakers is making a low-budget horror film in an abandoned hospital. In the course of doing so, they run into very real zombies and their undead master.

After a pre-credit sequence involving what appears to be a mad scientist, we see a female doctor is doing an autopsy on a corpse. As she investigates a neck wound, she discovers a tooth. She turns around for a second and, when she turns back to the table, the corpse is gone.

The corpse comes after the doctor and slashes her throat. It then throws her on the table and mounts her sexually, bringing her back to life in the process.

An off-screen voice yells for the scene to cut and we're introduced to the rest of the filmmakers. The director, David, has hired his two sisters, one of whom is the doctor who was just killed and reanimated, to work on the film. That sister, Shelly, is playing a role that his other sister, Nina, wanted for herself. Since she's funding the production, she's more than a bit annoyed that she wasn't cast in the role that she wanted.

The other players in the film—not the fictional production they're making—include Eric, the actor playing the corpse, Paul, a special effects tech, Topaz David's girlfriend who handles the production, and Marcus, who acts in the film and works as a PA.

David is soon involved in an argument with his sister, splitting up the group. While Topaz goes to recover everyone to get them back to work, she discovers the same room that appeared in the pre-credits video. She finds a videotape that was recorded by Dr. Eibon, the mad scientist character in the pre-credits sequence. She then finds what appears to be a coffin, made out of metal and covered in symbols. It has the flavor of a Frankenstein's laboratory, with the coffin being all wired into some sort of electrical apparatus and plenty of strange-looking equipment around.

They open up the coffin and the body of Dr. Eibon falls out. David thinks that the coffin will make a great prop and that using the corpse itself will add something new to his horror film.

They power up the machinery and, soon enough, Dr. Eibon and two zombies come out of the coffin and, on the doctor's orders, the zombies go after the crew. The crew runs around the hospital tries to get away from the zombies.

Dr. Eibon was a mad scientist, indeed, who wanted to bring his wife, who died of cancer, back to life. He began experimenting with the power of life and death and, of course, it went horribly wrong. He made his zombie henchmen but they hated the doctor because he was alive, so they threw him into the contraption he built.

It turns out that the device that Eibon created is more than just a machine. It opens up a portal to a hell-type dimension, and, in opening it the characters have brought some of that hell into their world and some of their world into that hell, leaving them trapped in a sort of in-between place. If this sounds a bit like the plot of *Hellraiser II*, the film doesn't try to argue against that. A Lament Configuration is shown sitting on Dr. Eibon's desk at one point. There are several other callouts to other horror films throughout this one, as well.

The zombies chase the crew through the hospital, with plenty of carnage along the way. There are some very slow moments of exposition, which is rather common in low-budget films; those scenes where the writers have characters explain what's happening rather than just showing it.

David, Topaz and Paul face off with Dr. Eibon on the graveyard set, which looks very much like an Ed Wood set. They use chainsaws and other weapons to fight off the undead, who rise from the fake graves, but the doctor and his minions catch Topaz and take her away.

Meanwhile, David and Paul disguise themselves as zombies using their makeup skills. They manage to get into the doctor's laboratory before he can complete his experiment on Topaz. Paul baits the zombies to go after him and manages to kill them with—obviously computer-generated—fire.

David finds a handgun and uses it to keep Dr. Eibon at bay. Paul returns and gets bitten by Zombie Shelly. He manages to kill her by sticking his thumbs in her eyes. David and Topaz face off with Dr. Eibon. Dr. Eibon gives a speech about how David and his crew are fools and how the dead cannot be stopped. David shoots Dr. Eibon in the head, which apparently stops him.

Paul has an extended death scene, at the end of which he tells David and Topaz to make a run for it as the zombies begin to crowd the hallway. They run off into the coffin apparatus, apparently crossing over into the hell dimension, where David resolves that they have to try to live.

Low-Budget and Derivative

Many great zombie films were low-budget affairs, including *Night of the Living Dead* and *28 Days Later*. This film is not anywhere near the caliber of either of those films, but it's a film made by people who love horror films and that much comes through.

The music in the film is oftentimes derivative of Christopher Young's score for *Hellraiser II*. It's almost comical, as Young's score was for a film that had epic themes and incredibly surreal imagery. Here, it comes off a bit overblown for the proceedings, but it's enough to get any serious horror fan close to the speakers wondering if they recycled the same music or just borrowed heavily in terms of the leitmotivs. The latter seems to be the case, judging by the information available about the film.

The film also references to Lucio Fulci, of course, given that it is a zombie film. There are other Easter egg references scattered throughout the film, too. While this film does suffer from its budgetary limitations and the occasional awful acting skills, it is fun to pore through it and try to discover which horror movie references they managed to squeeze in.

This is definitely a film that falls firmly in the low-budget category, so getting one's hopes up is highly inadvisable. There are some interesting elements to it, however, that are worth mentioning.

The Zombie Drought

Zombie films were far from popular at the time that this film was released and the genre was yet to rise from the grave as it did during the early 2000s. The zombies in this film, therefore, are derivative of the wave of zombie films that were popular in the 1970s and 80s.

The zombies are raised by supernatural means with scientific trappings, a la Frankenstein, as depicted in most of the films based on the book. They are, however, supernatural, by and large. Their master, Dr. Eibon, has the air of a Vodou master, with the zombies doing his bidding. They skip the mind control bit here, though, and opt for simpler forms of control, i.e., just ordering the zombies around.

The standout zombie is a green-faced monstrosity with lips that are rotted back to expose huge gums. It's no wonder he's pictured on the cover art. His look, and the look of the other zombies in this film, is one area where the filmmakers really come through. They also show that it doesn't take a lot of money to make a good screen zombie and, in fact, they give a step-by-step of the process in the scene where David and Paul are busy disguising themselves as the undead.

Two years after this film came out everything would change. For independent filmmakers, it's easy to see how the Romero-type zombies in this film are great antagonists. These slow-moving zombies don't require fast-chase choreography and, of course, because there's so much makeup involved, it's easy to reuse the same players over and over again. A few clever shots can turn five zombies into what appears to be an endless stream of them pouring through a hallway or doorway. The filmmakers did a good job of that here. The cheesy graveyard set also shows a genuine love of the genre, with Fulci's name appearing on one of the headstones.

The music includes tracks by Penis Flytrap, a band fronted by Dinah Cancer, formerly of 45 Grave, who did some of the music for *Return of the Living Dead*. This film was during a time when only hardcore fans would recognize most of the connections or even bothered to watch it, a fact that is referenced in the dialogue early on in the film. In that regard, it plays well as a fan piece made for a very specific demographic.

Enjoying These Zombies

The Dead Hate the Living! is not going to expose you to great filmmaking, or to storytelling that will stick with you the way that some zombie films do. This is a zombie film about zombie films, with plenty of references to other horror films thrown in. For horror aficionados who appreciate good, low-budget films—which are likely a lot of that demographic—this film should come through.

It's also interesting to see what amounts to one of the last gasps of the Romero zombies outside of Romero's own films and their remakes. By the time the full impact of *28 Days Later* was realized, zombies would be raging down the streets like professional sprinters, banging their way through doors and crawling through windows in a homicidal frenzy. In this film, they're still shambling down the hallways and there's plenty of time for a resourceful character to bait them into a trap.

The acting in this film is miles from great. The special effects, too, are lacking in most regards, though some of them are convincing and gory enough. Overall, this film wears its low budget on its sleeve and, if you enjoy films in that vein, this one should be a good time. If you prefer the more serious and plot-driven zombie films, and the much darker tones that have become popular over the later decades, this film will seem very light and flip, but it still could be good.

Expect a good time with this one—and some dull exposition—but don't expect it to be a great film. In the end, that's sort of the point!

28 Days Later (2002)

Director:

Danny Boyle

Starring:

Cillian Murphy

Naomie Harris

Christopher Eccleston

Megan Burns

Set in the UK, this film follows the journey of a bike messenger who wakes up to find that the zombie apocalypse has already taken down society and the entire UK is under quarantine. It's the film that's likely most responsible for making zombies popular film antagonists again. It won multiple awards and, of all the films featured in this book, this is one of the best. It's an absolute must-see.

The Plot

As this film opens up, we see a group of animal rights activists infiltrating a research lab. The reasons that they're there are obvious enough: animals are clearly being brutally tortured at this lab. As they get ready to set a group of chimps free, one of the researchers discovers them and tries to call for help. They stop him and the researcher pleads with them not to let the chimps go. They've been infected with something called "Rage"; it's in their blood and saliva and its effects are horrific.

One of the animal rights activists tries to coax a chimpanzee out of its cage. It flies out brutally mauls her. Soon after, she rises up, her eyes glowing red and attacks everyone else. Rage is out.

This results in the total evacuation of the UK. To protect the rest of the world, the UK is quarantined. What's left of the UK is an empty nation, save for a few survivors and hordes of infected.

The story switches to a man named Jim. He's laid out naked on a hospital bed when we first see him. It has been 28 days since the release of the Rage virus and Jim is just waking up from a coma. He was a bike messenger and got struck by a car. The hospital staff abandoned him, apparently, when they had to evacuate.

Jim wanders around empty hospital. Signs that it was abandoned in a hurry are all over, including overturned chairs, phones hanging off their cradles, and debris strewn about. Jim heads outside and finds largely the same situation. There is no one left. He finds a public bulletin board where people have posted pictures of the missing, but no one but Jim is there to see them.

Jim manages to make it to a church, where the former priest attacks him. He defends himself and injures the priest enough to get away, but still doesn't know what's going on. Two individuals who clearly know what they're doing, Selena and Mark, start throwing Molotov cocktails at the infected who begin to chase Jim. They cause a huge explosion and manage to get Jim to safety in the tubes beneath London.

Selena and Mark give Jim the lowdown on what has happened. Everything has fallen apart in the wake of Rage. The UK is empty and, as far as they know, the virus has spread beyond the UK, indicating that the entire world is falling apart.

Jim wants to find his parents, but discovers that they killed themselves, leaving Jim a note that they hoped to rejoin him in death, given that he was in a coma when the outbreak started. The infected discover Jim and his friends in the house and they are forced to flee. During the melee, Mark gets cut and blood from one of the infected contaminates the wound, forcing Selena to kill him.

Films of the Dead

They run into two more survivors, a cab driver named Frank and his daughter, Hannah. Frank is the epitome of the good guy character, offering shelter and to take off with Jim and Selena, since they don't have any way of surviving if they continue to hide out in the apartment building they've turned into their fortress.

Frank has discovered a radio beacon. It offers shelter and an answer to the infection. It appears to come from the military and Frank wants to go to the source of the signal to seek safety.

The group takes off in Frank's cab and make it out of the city. They endure attacks as they progress through the countryside. When they arrive at the blockade where the radio signal directs them, however, they find it apparently abandoned. In a rage, Frank shoots a crow perched on the blockade. A bit of blood falls into his eye and infects him. He tells Hannah to stay away from him, knowing it will take less than a minute before the infection claims him. Soldiers show up, sparing Frank's friends the trauma of having to kill Frank themselves.

The soldiers seem to be inviting at first, but the whole situation quickly starts to turn sinister. The man in charge of the operation, Major West, is warped. One of his men was infected and he keeps the man chained in the backyard. He believes that letting the zombies starve to death is the answer to infection and he's leaving his former solider to starve to death to get some idea of how long that will take.

West also plans to use Selena and Hannah to rebuild the population, ostensibly, but also points out that he promised his men women. Jim tries to get Hannah and Selena and run away from the base, but he's stopped. The women are given clothing to change into and the soldiers take them upstairs. They bring Jim and one of the soldiers who doesn't agree with what West is doing, Farrell. He and Jim are dragged out in the woods to be shot. One of the soldiers wants to stab Farrell to death with his bayonet, but the other objects. They shoot down Farrell but, as they do, Jim escapes. Jim climbs over the wall that surrounds the military camp and the soldiers assume that he'll die. They head back to base.

While Selena and Hannah are locked in the bedroom, Selena gives Hannah some drugs to psychologically protect her from the trauma of the rape she's inevitably going to endure. Jim, however, makes his way around to the front of the base and starts sounding an air raid siren. Two soldiers go out to get him, but Jim manages to get the drop on them. He goes back to the house and releases the infected that West has chained in the backyard to create a distraction. Jim manages to make it to Selena and Hannah, kills the guard that's watching them, and the three make a run for it. Jim gets shot by West, who was hiding in the back seat of their getaway vehicle. Hannah jumps in and backs up to the house, allowing the infected to break out the back window and get West. She picks up her two friends and they flee.

Selena has training as a pharmacist and they take Jim to a hospital, where she manages to treat his gunshot wound.

He goes back into another 28-day coma and awakens at a small, rural house. Selena is sewing.

In the final shots, they show Selena, Hannah, and Jim all putting the last part of "Hello," written in huge, sewn-together bed sheets, on the front lawn. A passing jet fighter sees the message and radios for help.

Reinventing the Genre

When the remake of *Dawn of the Dead* came out in 2004, many people debated whether the new, fast zombies were an improvement or a horrible mistake. *28 Days Later* is the film that gave us the first striking example of fast-moving zombies. It adds a lot of tension to the film, of course, but this film takes many risks that work in other ways, as well.

In many films of this sort, the survivors eventually have to figure out how the virus came to be, how to cure it, how to rebuild, and so forth. In this film, the characters are just trying to survive. They eventually figure out—after Jim sees jet flying over the military base—that the entire world hasn't been affected by Rage, so they do have hope. All they can do, however, is try to avoid any of the infected and, after their experience with Major West, any other human beings, long enough to signal for help and be evacuated out of the UK.

This could have amounted to an action film with a lot of chase and a little depth, but that doesn't happen. The film alternates between furious action scenes and reflective, almost dreamlike sequences. In one scene, for instance, after being chased by the infected, the characters end up at a farmhouse. They watch a group of apparently healthy horses run through a green field over a Brian Eno track. It's very odd and feels almost poetic but it's not long before the awfulness of the world bursts into the story again.

This film manages to say a lot without wasting time on a lot of exposition. The quiet moments in this film really stand out and are almost eerie at times. This brings up another element of this film that is way above average, particularly for the zombie film genre.

The music in this film is incredible. This would be a great film even with a lesser soundtrack, but the way the music is selected and used is way beyond what one normally sees in horror films. The piece of music that stands out as essentially the theme to the movie is "In the House, In a Heartbeat" by John Murphy. The piece starts out with a dreamy, psychedelic quality and constantly, incessantly builds and crescendos until it becomes anxiety-inducing. It's not always used as an obvious cue to let the audience know to get ready for an infected attack. Sometimes, such as at the beginning of the film when Jim sees the empty streets, it simply adds to the gravity of the moment.

This is one of the few zombie films that you don't have to forgive at any point. Most films in this genre have in-jokes or moments that are just meant to be light, like the celebrity look-alike undead shooting contest in the remake of *Dawn of the Dead*. This film doesn't have any of those elements. No matter what's going on, *28 Days Later* never lets you feel like things might be okay or that people could learn to deal with the zombie apocalypse for long enough to survive. This film's tone is post cannibalistic feast with a wildfire-rapid plague unleashed in the UK--We're following the last few survivors—or scraps of meat, as the case seems likely to be at times—trying to get out of the UK before they get killed. This movie, in short, isn't among those that make the zombie apocalypse look fun or like a action video game where you get to pick cool weapons, and shoot and chop your way to freedom. In this film, you're lucky if you make it a day, or even an hour.

About That Plague

Rage, the virus that starts the plague, is obviously playing on the rabies trope discussed in previous chapters. This virus is written to be frightening, however, and it doesn't come off as an exaggeration. The way the film is written makes the Rage plague seem all too realistic.

In the film, the research facility where the animal rights people break in is clearly some sort of covert operation. The conditions the animals are in and what they're subjected to are incredibly gruesome. One chimp is seen strapped to a table, dead, its chest cut away so that its ribs and abdomen could be examined. A living chimp is strapped to a table under a semi-circle of screens that play loops of violent imagery. This is clearly some sort of a military operation from the start. The Rage virus, if it only attacked a specific population, would be a devastating biological warfare agent.

When the virus breaks out, what happens is not completely unrealistic. Some infections come on incredibly fast. Rage is one of them. After being exposed, it takes around 30 seconds for the infection to wreak havoc on the person's brain, turning them completely homicidal. It spreads easily through bites, and the infected attack anyone and anything they see without fear or hesitation. They are, in the commonly understood if not clinical definition of the term, rabid.

This rabies-like plague spreads within days and, with such a fast rate of infection and such unbridled violence, society has collapsed within weeks of the outbreak. Jim was, odd as it is to say, lucky he was in a coma at the time it was spreading. However, he was not lucky in that he couldn't be taken along when everyone evacuated.

This plague is frightening because, as well as being based on a real-world boogeyman like rabies, it doesn't require anything supernatural to occur. The zombies in this film aren't dead; they're infected. They're still living people. The film manages to avoid the consequences of shooting sick, rather than undead, people by making them completely and utterly inhuman in their behavior. The virus fundamentally changes them, and there's no going back.

While West may be deranged, his idea of the answer to stopping the infection is not far-fetched at all. It makes sense that, since the zombies are alive, they would starve after a while and finding out how long that's going to take makes perfect strategic sense. There's no other way to kill them off so adopting the mentality required to outlast a siege makes sense. West's deranged behavior is a result of him not believing that the end has already come; it is not a result of him being truly evil.

The plague is also demonstrated to be understandable, partially thanks to West, which further removes the story from the supernatural. There are too many infected to kill and the infection spreads too quickly and easily to safely take them on, but they are still alive and, like anything else that's alive, they'll starve to death without food. They have no capacity, as West points out, to build a future, so it's inevitable that they're not going to last and that waiting them out might work. There's a point to doing the hard work of surviving in this film, in short, which isn't true in some other zombie films, where it's implied that everything is gone forever, as far as anyone can tell.

Get the DVD

Like any good story, there are several revisions and versions of this one. They're included on the DVD release of the film and are worth seeing. They all take a different turn as to the main elements of the story, particularly the one that was never even filmed. As dark as this film is—and it is very dark—the ending the filmmakers eventually went with was more hopeful than some of their other endings were. The fact that it's lighter doesn't detract from the film at all and, arguably, some of the other endings were so dark that it might have made the film less satisfying.

If you're a true zombie fan, having the DVD of this film is well worth the cost increase over just streaming it. This film has real depth, and it's worth exploring the other ways that it could have gone and getting to enjoy the rest of the extras.

Enjoying These Zombies

It's not exaggerating the matter to say that, at some point in the future, someone will probably be telling a younger zombie fan about how *28 Days Later* is really just as important as Romero's films in zombie canon. This is the film that decided to crank up the speed on zombies to terrifying effect. It's also among the films that managed to completely take the supernatural element out of the zombie apocalypse and, even more importantly, to give it a realistic possible cause.

This film has an impressive 87% rating from critics on Rotten Tomatoes—no small feat. It's a good film all around and, for those who love zombie films, it will be apparent that this makes *28 Days Later* something of a standout.

This film had a budget of around $8,000,000, certainly not in high-budget territory. The cast weren't famous when the film was released, which is actually something of a strength for horror films.

The filmmakers were incredibly creative with what they had to work with and the performances are excellent. Every bit of this film looks like it had thought put into it. The interspersing of the very dreamlike sequences with the harsh action is extremely effective and, once the soundtrack is on top of it all, it's really a masterpiece.

The gore and violence in this film are used in a way that's never gross-out level and that always functions to show that there is real danger to the characters in this story. The violence is brutal. The infected really are terrifying and, when they attack, it's obvious how Rage spread so quickly. In films where the zombies are slow, you can get ahead of them, but between the speed with which these zombies move and the fact that the plague they carry infects the host almost instantly, it's not hard to imagine how Rage could have brought down society.

All of that taken into account, it's clear that this is a zombie film for grownups. This film knows how to make you afraid of the infected just as *Night of the Living Dead* knew how to make you afraid of the undead.

Before *28 Days Later* came out, zombie films were mostly outdated and really not scary. They had become a bit like vampire films are right now, with most of the fear factor being removed and the characters being laughable as threats, for the most part.

28 Days Later made zombies scary again. *Resident Evil* came out during the same year and, even though that movie did feature updated zombies, they don't really hold a candle to the zombies in this film. The infected are probably the most convincing zombie threat of the early 21st century and, if you're enjoying the new wave of zombie films that have come around over the last several years, then you have these filmmakers to thank to a great degree. Get this film. You won't be disappointed.

Resident Evil (2002)

Director:

Paul W.S. Anderson

Starring:

Milla Jojovich

Michelle Rodriguez

Eric Mabius

Resident Evil is based on a video game series of the same name. The film follows the protagonist, Alice, as she discovers who she is and what horrible things the Umbrella Corporation has been up to. This is the first installment in a series that includes several sequels.

The Plot

The plot of this film includes most of the major elements from the video game series. It takes place in Raccoon City. The city is home to a research facility called The Hive, which is run by the Umbrella Corporation. The Hive is a multi-floor facility that's almost entirely underground, where top-secret research is conducted and, as it happens, where medical and scientific ethics are generally absent.

The facility is developing a virus called the T-virus. At the outset of the film, this virus is stolen and gets out into the facility.

To contain the contamination, the Red Queen, the name for the highly developed artificial intelligence that runs The Hive's security, seals off the facility. It further kills anyone in the facility and releases a gas that causes amnesia, erasing the memories of any survivors.

Alice, played by Jovovich, finds herself in an opulent but empty mansion. She cannot remember who she is or how she got there.

She's attacked but, before her assailant can flee, a group of operatives wearing gas masks descends on the mansion. They arrest Addison, who attacked Alice.

Alice learns that she is an employee of the Umbrella Corporation, though she has no recollection of it. She is in charge of protecting one of the entrances to The Hive research facility. She's supposed to be working with a man named Spence, posing as a couple.

The operatives are trying to figure out why The Hive was shut down. They need to get into the facility and take Alice with them. They find Spence and all head into the facility via a private train system located underneath the mansion.

The Red Queen still has the facility locked down. The operatives try to get into the control center for the artificial intelligence, but it's protected by a system of lasers that slice through anyone who tries to get down the hall leading to the control room. Alice manages to evade the lasers, demonstrating that she's clearly had some sort of advanced training and is exceptionally athletic.

In disabling the Red Queen, the crew also takes down the security system at The Hive, releasing the zombies, which have turned after being exposed to the virus. The virus is passed along as it is in many other films: via bite. One of the squad, Rain, gets bitten when they first encounter the zombies.

Matt, who was posting as a police officer, turns out to have been one of a brother-and-sister team of environmental activists that was trying to infiltrate The Hive. Alice starts to remember being one of their contacts. She also remembers that, as a condition of helping the activists, she insisted that the Umbrella Corporation be brought down. There are still blanks to fill in, however.

The team and Alice, or what remains of them, have to escape The Hive; it has an additional shut-down sequence that permanently seals it off and there are 60 minutes for them to get out.

Films of the Dead ■ 193

On the way out, Alice remembers that Spence, her faux-boyfriend, was behind the entire outbreak of the T-virus. He engineered the release so that he could cover himself getting out of the facility with a quantity of it.

The group tries to get away on a train, but Rain succumbs to her bite and becomes a zombie. A mutant attacks the train, giving the group one last huge fight before they're free.

Alice and Matt are the only survivors. Alice wakes up from being knocked out long enough to see men from Umbrella coming to take Matt away and that Matt is starting to mutate. They mention the "Nemesis" program—a hook for the sequel—and Alice gets knocked out again and wakes up in a hospital.

There doesn't seem to be anyone around and her memory is gone again. She sneaks out of the hospital and goes out on the street, to see that the city has been destroyed. The buildings are all empty and abandoned vehicles clog the streets. A newspaper headline is shown that reveals a zombie apocalypse has already taken place, due to the virus making it out of The Hive.

Alice takes off into the chaos.

Good or Not?

Resident Evil, as was pointed out, is based on the video game series of the same name. This is a video game movie that includes zombies, not a zombie movie that is based on a video game.

With that in mind, *Resident Evil* is not bad. It plays out a bit like a video game. The main character—the player analogue—is given a sketch of the story, a mystery to solve and a series of challenges that they have to live through. As Alice goes through The Hive, she proves herself a very good—superhuman, in fact—fighter. She gets better as she works her way through the facility, essentially leveling up. As she and Matt exit the facility, they do battle with one of the licker mutants that's much more powerful than anything they've fought before. Fortunately, there's only the one creature to fight, which makes it, essentially, a boss fight.

If you're a gamer, this film will probably appeal to you. The format will be familiar and the style of shooting and the way the action sequences are done are good. Milla Jovovich has a huge following among geeky audiences and, if you're in that demographic, you'll probably like this movie.

That said, out of the five movies in the *Resident Evil* franchise, this film has the highest rating on Rotten Tomatoes, at 33 percent.

Among audiences, however, this film has a 68 percent rating.

Whether it's good or not, it does have zombies and its own unique place for them within the plot.

The Zombies

The zombies in *Resident Evil* are created by exposure to the T-virus. The T-virus is treated in a fashion similar to how radiation is treated in many '50s and '60s monster and horror films. It can kill people, turn them into mutants of a sort and, in this case, it turns people into zombies. No matter what it turns people into, those mutations or zombies are immediately hostile toward the living.

The human zombies in this film are generally of the slower variety. They can be killed by massive damage or headshots, following the conventions of most zombies. There are also zombie dogs, which have been mutated further by the virus.

The zombies provide some of the menace in this film, largely following the convention of the shambling sort of zombies that attack en masse. When they become mutated, however, the mutants are dangerous enough that fighting even one of them is inadvisable.

The final boss fight involves a mutated creature called a "licker," distinguished by a long tongue and a dog-like shape. Alice shows herself to be much stronger, faster and more resilient in this and other fights. She's clearly human, however, and she shows compassion for the members of the team. When the Red Queen makes killing off Rain, who has been contaminated by a zombie bite, a condition of leaving the facility, Alice can't bring herself to do it.

The zombie mutagen is contagious in this film, giving it elements of films with plague zombies. They're also undead, which has a supernatural angle. The mutations fit into the current social anxieties regarding genetic tampering and other advanced processes. Those anxieties also make for great monsters, of course, and the mutations in this film are memorable.

The zombies aren't quite so memorable, but, throughout this series, they'll remain a source of background menace. As the franchise goes on, it involves more and more developed mutants and Alice shows herself to be obviously a bit too athletic and resilient to be a normal human being.

Enjoying These Zombies

These zombies will appeal most to gamers. If your most frequent zombie encounters are in *Resident Evil, Killing Floor, Left 4 Dead* and other video game franchises built around those monsters, it's almost certain that you'll enjoy this film, at least for the fights.

Be aware, however, that the film diverges significantly from the plot and storyline of the video games. According to Game Front, this film was originally conceived as a prequel to the video games. The writers didn't want people to be bored with the film, since they'd know its content going in if it was a direct adaptation of the game content.

For those who want a deep story that focuses on zombies and the effects of the zombie apocalypse, the movie is not likely to be that enjoyable. Likewise, for people who want a story that offers a great degree of realism within a horror film. This film is a horror, science fiction and action film in equal measures, but not really much of a drama.

If you appreciate this film, you're likely to appreciate Milla Jovovich's performance. She's very good at the physical stuff and that's largely what this film demands of her. She doesn't have to establish herself as a protagonist, as the audience is introduced to her in the same way they'd be introduced to their character in an RPG video game, in many regards. We know she's the one who's going to survive whatever goes on in The Hive and beyond. The enjoyable element of this film is watching Alice survive, not wondering if she's really going to make it.

The zombies are some, but not all, of the threat. There's never any doubt whether or not Alice can best them. In video game parlance, the zombies in this film are essentially "trash mobs." They're easy enough to kill or outwit, but there are a lot of them.

This film is interesting in that it does twist the usually Evil Corporation trope around a bit. Umbrella was developing this virus, true, but it seemed to be willing to do anything up to and including killing its own employees to keep the virus contained. It also seemed to be quite capable of containing it, given the complexity and security in The Hive. As the Game Front article and others have pointed out, it's really Spence that's to blame for everything that goes wrong due to the release of the virus. The Umbrella Corporation seemed to take the virus seriously enough to give it a great deal of protection. It was simple greed that set it loose in the world.

This film is part of a five-film—to date—franchise and people who like this film will probably like the later installments. They move further and further from the narrative of the video game so you won't necessarily know what's coming even if you've played through all the *Resident Evil* games.

Like films based on comic books, this film won't be for everyone. Also like films based on comic books, some people will probably really enjoy *Resident Evil* and its sequels. It's worth giving it a chance and, keep in mind, audiences generally like this film, even if critics do not.

Doom (2005)

Director:

Andrzej Bartkowiak

Starring:

Dwayne "The Rock" Johnson

Karl Urban

Rosamund Pike

Doom is not a great film by any stretch, but neither is *Plan 9 from Outer Space* and *Plan 9* is certainly worth watching. This film is based on a video game franchise, an FPS zombie/mutant shooter by id Software. For fans of the game and fans of zombie shootouts, this film will deliver. For fans of engaging stories, plot consistency and great writing, it won't deliver, but still has the potential to be a very good time.

The Plot

The plot of *Doom* is very barebones, owing to its videogame origins. The United Aerospace Corporation (UAC) is the Evil Corporation in this film. The good guys consist of a squadron of Marines and a scientist who may not be revealing everything she knows about the research that she's doing for UAC.

In the beginning of the film, a scientist is sending out a distress call and order to quarantine the Olduvai Research Facility, which is located on Mars. He's attacked, but we don't get to see who or what his attacker is.

The Marines are getting ready to go on leave and are led by Asher Mahonin, who is called "Sarge". He has a group of men who spend most of their time insulting and berating one another. The dialogue is pretty much relegated to sex jokes, challenging someone's masculinity and so forth.

Humans use a technology called the Ark to get back and forth from Mars. The team is dispatched through the Ark to investigate the happenings at the research facility.

One member of the team, who goes by the name "Reaper," has a sister at the station. She's an archaeologist and Sarge doesn't want Reaper to go because of the presence of his sister. Reaper goes anyway.

The team finds out that the archeologists discovered the remains of the creatures that used to live on Mars. They are vaguely humanoid, but much smaller. They also have 24 chromosomes instead of 23. This is apparently engineered and gave the creatures enhanced physiology and mental abilities.

The Marines soon run into the scientists who were attacked. They've turned into mutant zombies. This is the first confrontation of the film, which is largely built around the battle scenes.

The team fights off several mutants and loses several of their own men. The zombies have clearly taken over the base, so Sarge orders a complete evacuation. Two doctors stay behind to assist with the Ark.

Reaper's sister—Dr. Grimm—investigates the dead bodies and finds out that they're mutated human beings. The team finds out there are missing scientists among the dead and, given what Dr. Grimm has discovered, has to assume the worst.

Sarge levels up his weapon with the BFG 9000, a gigantic gun that shoots devastating rounds. They're after the Hell Knight, one of the creatures from the video game franchise. The monster tears through the Marines and several chases ensue.

It turns out that the scientists were actually trying to replicate what the aliens had done with genetic engineering and that their experiments had gone awry. A prisoner who was convicted of multiple murders and sentenced to death was used as a test subject. He is the Hell Knight. The team has to make sure that the Hell Knight doesn't make it back to Earth and, to make thing worse, he's already trying to get to the Ark. There's a good-and-evil element to all of it, as well. The zombies look for people with tendencies to be evil and try to avoid anyone with tendencies to be good.

Sarge decides, after several more people are discovered slaughtered by the Hell Knight, to kill anyone else remaining on the base. He doesn't differentiate between the infected and the well. He sends out his men but one of his Marines returns and reports that there are several survivors hidden away in a closet and that he's not going to kill them. Sarge shoots the dissenter.

The rest of Sarge's crew rebel, but the Hell Knight stops the situation from exploding when it launches an attack. It's followed up by a group of zombies. Reaper gets hurt and, to save him, his sister gives him an injection that contains the mutagen.

The mutagen works and Reaper becomes super-powered, but retains his humanity. The sequence that follows mirrors the first-person perspective of the game, with Reaper gunning down mutants as he runs through a hallway. At the end of what amounts to the level, he encounters his boss fight, Sarge. The two fight an epic battle, but Reaper gets the best of Sarge by tossing him through the Ark. He then tosses a grenade through the device, which kills him and disables the transporter.

So Bad It's Good

Some zombie films—*28 Days Later, Night of the Living Dead*—are masterpieces. *Doom* is not one of those films. Nonetheless, it can be a lot of fun if you watch it with the right attitude.

If you're a fan of the game or of zombie run-and-guns in general, you'll likely get into *Doom*. It follows the video game formula very closely. More on that below.

Even if you're not a fan of the video games, you'll likely get a good laugh out of some of the lines in this film. There are some classics, including: "If they were so smart, how come they're so dead?"; "Ten percent of the human genome is still unmapped. Some say it's the genetic blueprint for the soul"; and "I'm not supposed to die," uttered by Sarge as he seems to be getting killed far too early for plot convenience.

This isn't a great film. It has horrible reviews from audiences and critics alike. Then again, it is what it's supposed to be: dumb fun. It has plenty of action sequences and, if you're a gamer, you'll spot the tropes that they follow right away.

The Video Game Element

This film shares with *Resident Evil* origins in a video game. *Doom*, the video game, is one of the most famous games of all, starting out all the way back in 1993. The game was a first-person shooter and among the most important of that genre. To understand parts of *Doom*, the movie, you have to understand something about *Doom*, the game.

The game features a character that is basically identical to the Marines in the film. An evil force is let through portals much like the Ark in the film and the point of the game is, basically, for the character "Doomguy" to figure out what's happening as he shoots his way through the evil creatures that come through the gateway.

In these video games, and others that it influenced, the player usually sees the backside of the weapon that they're carrying, their character's hands, and the environment according to whichever way they're facing. As they progress through levels, they get better weapons and the occasional boost. These would be the BFG and the injection with the mutagen in the film, respectively.

The sequence where Reaper runs through the hallways after being genetically enhanced are nearly exactly what you'd see if you were playing *Doom*. The intent of this film is clear and so is its target audience. If you've never had a desire to see *Doom* the game made into a film, you probably won't like this film.

Enjoying These Zombies

Doom is clunky; the dialogue is sometimes awful and sometimes funny. The action sequences are well done, however, which is good since they're the centerpieces of the film.

The characters are the same as any military character in any macho military action film: rude, abusive toward one another, and have the sense of humor of a teenage boy. The one who stands out is Reaper, who's clearly intelligent—relatively intelligent, more accurately—and who presents the only threat to the biggest boss of all, The Rock.

Doom, like many films that aren't well written, has a plot that can be very hard to follow. It's also a plot that randomly uses scientific information to motivate aspects of the story, but that doesn't seem to have spent a lot of time thinking them through. For example, the way in which someone is given an extra chromosome is not made clear, nor is there a reason given for why a person's body would suddenly re-grow itself into something different.

The zombies in this film are of the mutant variety, but they are mixed up with concepts of good and evil in that becoming infected doesn't necessarily mean becoming a threat. In fact, if you're a good person, being infected apparently makes you a better person. These aren't zombies the way you'll see them in most films, and in fact, they're similar to the sorts of zombies you see in most video games. They're faster, aren't really the walking dead so much as they are the altered dead. Half the point of them even existing is to get blown up, set on fire, shot, or attacked with a chainsaw.

Doom is great if you want to watch a bad, but fun, movie. If you're not interested in that kind of movie-watching, skip it.

Dawn of the Dead (2004)

Director:

Zack Snyder

Starring:

Sarah Polley

Ving Rhames

Jake Weber

This film is a remake of the 1978 George A. Romero classic, featured in an earlier chapter. For the most part, it follows the same story, but in a setting that is more modern and with a level of darkness that wasn't really seen much in film in the 1970s.

The Plot

This film doesn't open up like the original *Dawn of the Dead*. The zombie apocalypse is not in full swing yet and, in fact, there are only some hints that something is about to go wrong. We start out following Ana, who works in a hospital. There have been strange things going on with the patients, but nothing so out of the ordinary that there's any sort of panic over it.

Ana goes home and, along the way, we're introduced to her neighbor's daughter, Vivian Ana joins her husband, Louis

The television starts playing an emergency broadcast, but neither of them see it and both end up falling asleep after having sex.

In the morning, Vivian shows up at their bedroom door. She appears to be injured, with blood all around her mouth and Louis tries to help. She attacks Louis, biting deep into his neck. Ana throws her off and tosses her back down the hallway.

Vivian jumps to her feet and runs, full speed, back toward Ana. Louis dies but comes back to life soon after and goes after Ana.

Ana escapes and tries to flee the neighborhood. It's obvious that everything is falling apart quickly. She manages to get out of the neighborhood, but gets into a crash. When she wakes up, Kenneth is there, a Milwaukee cop who has managed to hang onto his firearms. The two take off together and soon meet up with a trio of people. Andre and Luda are a couple. Luda is pregnant.

They figure out what's going on, at least as far as the dead rising up and attacking the living is concerned. They decide to hide out in a mall. They manage to get through the zombies they encounter and to get inside.

There are already people inside the mall, however. The security guards have been hiding out inside and are not immediately welcoming to Ana and her friends. More survivors arrive the next day. This group includes a father and daughter, an older woman, and several other people. The woman, who has been bitten already, dies. When she comes back, the group figures out that anyone who is bitten dies and is then resurrected as a zombie.

One of the other survivors has been bitten but has not yet died. The group knows that he's going to turn, but Kenneth sits with him while he waits to die. When Frank finally does expire, Kenneth finishes him off to keep the others safe.

There is one more person who's been bitten: Luda, who is also pregnant. Her bite, however, is not significant and it doesn't seem to be affecting her, at least not right away.

The group seems to enjoy the comforts of the mall, at least for a time. As in the first film, they amuse themselves by using anything and everything they find in the mall. The power goes out, however,

Films of the Dead

forcing some of the survivors to leave the safe area so that they can get power restored to the facility.

There is a survivor across the street from the mall, Andy, who runs a gun store. He and Kenneth begin to forge a friendship of sorts from a distance. When Bart, Michael, Kenneth, and CJ, the leader of the security guards, go down to turn the power back on, they're attacked and Bart is killed.

Luda's wound continues to get worse and, eventually, she turns into a zombie. She's about to deliver and her husband, Andre, ties her to a bed and delivers the child, who is born undead.

Norma figures out what's going on and kills her. Andre goes after Norma and the two kill one another. Ana is forced to kill off the undead child.

Realizing that they cannot stay at the mall forever, the survivors try to hash out a plan. One of their number, Steve, is a—very entitled—wealthy individual and has access to a yacht. They decide that they should try to make it to the yacht, which they can take out on the water to safety.

The group decides to armor-up two busses in the basement for the job. Andy is running out of supplies fast, however, and the group try to get him food before he dies.

Nicole, one of the survivors, has bonded with a dog named Chips. The zombies don't seem to be interested in anything other than human beings, so the other survivors reason that sending Chips over with food could save Andy.

They send the dog over, but it ends up catching the attention of one of the zombies, who slips into Andy's gun shop along with the dog. Andy kills the zombie, but gets bitten in the process.

Nicole steals a truck and goes to the gun shop to rescue the dog. She crashes the vehicle and gets inside, hiding out from Andy, who's now a zombie. CJ, Kenneth, and a few of the other survivors go over to rescue her. Kenneth kills zombie Andy. They crawl through a sewer to get back but Tucker breaks his legs climbing down. CJ tries to drag him to safety, but the zombies catch up and CJ has to shoot Tucker to keep him from being devoured alive.

Steve, who's shown himself to be remarkably selfish, locks Kenneth and the group out, but Ana intervenes and lets them in. The zombies are at their door and they have to get to the boat.

As they ply the busses through the huge crowds of zombies, CJ starts improvising explosives by shooting propane tanks. In the second bus, Glen tries to use a chainsaw through slits in the side of the bus to keep zombies back. He slips when the bus gets jolted and saws into Monica, killing her. Glen dies when the bus crashes. Steven gets attacked as he tries to get away.

The group in the first bus goes back and saves the survivors of the second. Ana fulfills a sarcastic promise she made to Steve earlier in the film when she kills his zombified version by shooting him in the head.

The group makes it to the marina, crashing the bus into the dock. They make a run for the boat but, seeing that they're not going to make it, CJ tells them to go without him. He fights some of the zombies off before detonating another propane tank and killing a large number of them.

Michael tells the group he's been bitten and refuses to get on the boat, knowing he's going to turn. He helps them shove off and the remaining survivors, consisting of Michael, Terry, Chips, Nicole, Kenneth, and Ana, sail off into Lake Michigan. Michael kills himself back on shore.

As the credits roll, short pieces of footage from a video camera on the boat play. They show Steve partying on the boat in better times, intercut with scenes of the group sailing around Lake Michigan. Their food and fuel run out, but the group finds an island and decides to explore it. Before they can, a horde of zombies rushes the boat.

Films of the Dead

The camera drops and we see a series of zombie faces looking at it, leaving it unclear as to what happened to the survivors.

Faster and More Violent

Many modern remakes of films tend to be faster paced and darker than the originals on which they were based. This one is no exception. Compared to the 1978 *Dawn of the Dead*, the action in this film is more violent and more intense. This has not been without controversy among fans.

While *Resident Evil* and *28 Days Later* both had fast zombies, this is the film that most people likely associate with starting the trend. Presumably, this is because these zombies are, in most regards, Romero zombies on fast-forward. They're incredibly aggressive and relentless attackers and quickly form a large horde when any kind of noise attracts their attention.

This film has plenty of outstanding zombie attack scenes, but the standout one is the very first one where Ana flees her home. In this sequence, Ana takes her car and tries to get out of her neighborhood. A radio plays, alerting her that the wave of murder and rioting have affected all of the areas surrounding Milwaukee.

Ana's neighborhood is quickly becoming a war zone. When she asks what's going on, a neighbor pulls a gun on her and tells her to stay away. As she flees in her car, a zombie begins to chase her and, seeing the neighbor, peels off and tackles him in his yard. This is all moving incredibly fast. It's not the same buildup that occurs in Romero's film, where the zombies gradually start to overwhelm areas. These zombies move fast, take out anyone they see immediately, and, as the zombie chasing Ana's car demonstrates, are capable of running much faster than humans.

The characters in this film are very much updated from the first film. In the first film, the characters have been dealing with the zombie apocalypse for some time. They take off with a qualified helicopter pilot and two SWAT team members, giving them ample resources in the way of transportation and muscle. In this film, the characters are mostly regular people. Ana is a nurse, so she has medical skills that will obviously become useful. Kenneth is a cop and a tough one. Other than that, however, the characters aren't terribly remarkable. These are 21st-century people, however, and there's a noticeable difference in how they deal with the zombie apocalypse compared to the characters in the first film.

The characters in the remake seem more or less comfortable with the idea—as much as one can be—that society is collapsing. Andre, a former criminal with a pregnant wife, expresses to Kenneth his desire to give his kid everything he never had. Even with society collapsing, these people see themselves surviving.

Steve is a very 21st-century character, as well. He's not horrified by the zombie apocalypse, and, in fact, seems to be somewhat bored with it. He treats it as something that had the nerve to interfere with his notions of entitlement. Steve, to put it in parlance that would become popular a few years after this film came out, is an economic one percent-er. He's an arrogant, self-serving, and shortsighted person, but he has a boat, so the other characters keep him alive as best they can in order to use it to escape.

The main characters in this film are Ana, Kenneth, and Michael. While Ana and Kenneth have zombie apocalypse-friendly skills, Michael is a television salesman at Best Buy. What's interesting here is that, even though this is the case, he ends up being one of the most important—and capable—characters. In the 21st century, the reality of life is that many people are employed in jobs that don't allow them to demonstrate what they have to offer. The zombie apocalypse does that for Michael, but at a horrible cost.

In this film, in fact, a lot of the characters end up surprising us. CJ starts out as a very cynical person, and in many regards, the character is set up as an antagonist. In the end, however, he proves to be among the most heroic of all the characters and becomes very likeable. Kenneth seems not to care about much of anything other than finding his brother, but once he finds out the camp has been destroyed and all the people there are now "dead-ish," according to Steve, he adopts the group of survivors as at least friends, if not family.

Is It Better than the Original?

Dawn of the Dead is a low-budget remake of a low-budget film. Both of them show their low budgets in various ways. In the remake, for instance, some of the CGI effects are a bit lacking, such as the helicopter shot of Ana's suburb, where some of the houses don't actually have driveways that connect to the road. However, the filmmakers did a great job of allocating the resources they had to the shots that mattered. In the finale sequence, the hordes of zombies look very real and the flight in the fortified busses is intense and well done.

In the original film, the low budget comes through in the form of zombies that don't really look dead, just covered in green paint. Romero manages to make this not matter at all by having plenty of gore effects that are convincing enough to be revolting. You might notice that some of the zombies are a bit unconvincing, in other words, but you'll change your mind once they start tearing a character limb from limb and your brain focuses on the horror of the moment rather than the makeup.

In the remake, the filmmakers have the zombies move quickly and aggressively. In the scenes where the CGI is a bit lacking, the staging of the action usually more than makes up for it. In the neighborhood scenes, for instance, the action is so fast once it gets going that it's impossible not to get involved. The running scenes are particularly well done in this film, and the first time Ana gets attacked is quite memorable.

These zombies, like Romero's zombies, rise quickly after being killed. The big difference is that they also move quickly.

This movie is really neither better nor worse than the original. It's more modern. It has plenty of tributes to the original film in it in the form of Easter eggs. A helicopter that flies by the camera at one point, for instance, is the same helicopter that appears in the original *Dawn of the Dead*. The names of various characters from the original show up on shop signs and so forth. Fans that want to dig that deeply into this film will find plenty to keep them happy.

Enjoying These Zombies

Some people really didn't like this film. Take a look at most of the, however, and you'll find that many of them just amount to the same sort of nitpicking that passes for movie criticism now that anyone and everyone can publish themselves online.

In the above-linked article, the author mentions that it might be unbelievable that Ana and her husband don't realize that a state of emergency is on until they wake up in the morning. This is actually a bit silly. They have sex in the shower and pass out together in bed without watching television or listening to the radio. They live in a suburb where nothing is really happening until they get up in the morning. It actually seems perfectly logical that they might not know what's going on until they wake up.

People have nitpicked plenty of other things as well, but it really just amounts to discouraging people from seeing a decent zombie flick. If all movies were realistic, no one would score a running headshot on a zombie, most of the characters would simply get exhausted and overwhelmed if they had to fight hand-to-hand, and illness, hunger, and thirst would likely wipe out the characters that did manage to take shelter. The whole plot of any one of these movies is entirely unrealistic, so it's best to take *Dawn of the Dead* for what it is: a zombie film.

In that regard, it does well both as a remake and a standalone film. The action is well choreographed and the characters that are clearly not fit enough to survive die quickly, as they would in real life. The characters have between them a handy blend of skills and experience, but no one is conveniently a Navy SEAL or a brilliant surgeon. These are regular people and they're relatable.

One of the things that people really liked about the original *Dawn of the Dead* is that Romero developed his characters more than is usually the case in horror films. It was hard to watch some of them die, even after they made stupid decisions that rendered their deaths inevitable. It's the same in this film. When Tucker dies, it's sad, as he's really a likeable and capable character. When Norma, Luda, and Andre all kill one another, it's equally tragic and fully reasonable to see both Andre's and Norma's motivations for doing what they do. Even Andy, who doesn't appear on-screen except for through binoculars, ends up being a likeable character.

This film is worth seeing for anyone who likes zombie films. The original *Dawn of the Dead* holds up, for certain, but it does show its age in many regards. The men are overly macho, the CB-chatter scene is likely strange to anyone born after 1980, and the slow-moving zombies are sinister, but they're the sinister of the past, not the present.

The zombies in the remake aren't like the zombies in the first film, but they capture the spirit of what that film did. This film makes the classic Romero-type zombie frightening again. No one knows exactly why or how they're rising from the dead and whether the world will survive them or not. The point is to provide the audience with characters that they care enough about to want to see survive and to make sure that there is plenty of reason to be afraid along the way. This film succeeds in both of those regards.

As many of the articles and reviews of this movie show, it's far too easy to say that something isn't as good as the original, make some nitpicky comments about it, and call it a valid criticism. This film deserves more respect than that. If anything, this film shows that the filmmakers had some regard for the original and were, in all likelihood, fans. After all, only someone who really liked the original *Dawn of the Dead* would understand the significance of the helicopter to the story and the fact that the mall was more than a shelter and was something of a character in itself.

Even if you're a die-hard Romero fan, give this film a chance. If you have and didn't like it, give it another one with fresh eyes. There's a lot to like here.

One significant, and ironic, advantage that this film has over some other modern zombie films is that it doesn't have sequels, as of yet. It doesn't attempt to set up a complex narrative about the origins of the zombies, either. It takes it for granted that the zombies are a threat, puts people at risk of being attacked by them, and lets the story unfold from there. In those regards, it works.

The acting in this movie is good, the action is well directed and staged, and the effects—particularly the zombie gore—are very convincing. It's not an abandoning of what Romero created and, in fact, it shows that the living dead stories he crafted have cross-generational appeal to such an extent that people still want to see his stories played out on-screen, even if they're updated a bit here and there.

Shaun of the Dead (2004)

Director:

Edgar Wright

Starring:

Simon Pegg

Nick Frost

Kate Ashfield

Shaun of the Dead is one of the best zombie comedies out there. The film manages to provide characters that are interesting outside of the zombie apocalypse they end up having to survive. This is very much a black comedy, and plenty of gruesome deaths take place within its runtime. Somehow, it manages to make it all very amusing to watch.

The Plot

Shaun is what Americans would call a slacker. He lives in London and works at an electronics store, where some of the employees call him grandpa, even though he's only 29 years old. He has a girlfriend, Liz, who wants Shaun to do more with his life. He also has a friend, Ed, who lives on Shaun's couch, plays video games, drinks a lot, and annoys Shaun's roommate, Pete.

Shaun's parents consist of his mother, Barbara, and his stepfather, Phillip. Shaun gets on well with Ed and fairly well with Barbara, but most of the other people in his life think he's just wasting his time and should aim a bit higher.

A friend, Yvonne, reminds Shaun that it's his and Liz's anniversary. Shaun realizes he forgot all about it and didn't come through on his promise to get them a reservation at a restaurant that they both like. He tries to get the reservation, but it's too late and Liz dumps him.

Films of the Dead

Shaun and Ed to go their favorite pub, The Winchester, to have some drinks. They get very drunk, come home at four in the morning and start blasting records, waking up Shaun's roommate. Shaun has to intervene to stop Pete from beating Ed up, and Pete reveals that he got mugged by crackheads on his way home and that one of them bit him.

Shaun wakes up in the middle of the zombie apocalypse, but he doesn't know it yet. He's slept in, has a hangover, and flips through television stations urgently warning of the wave of zombie attacks. Ed comes in and tells Shaun that there's a woman in their backyard. They believe that she's drunk, as she's very slow-moving and clumsy. Of course, she's a zombie. She keeps trying to attack Shaun until he shoves her back. She falls, impales herself on a post, and gets right back up.

Shaun and Ed listen to the news long enough to find out that the only way to kill off what they now have figured out are zombies is to decapitate them or to damage the brain. They go back out and try to kill the zombie, who has now been joined by another, by throwing things at them. They resort to using Shaun's record collection—selecting them based on quality and lamenting the destruction of an original pressing of New Order's *Blue Monday*—until Shaun finally breaks into the shed in their backyard and retrieves a cricket bat. Ed gets a shovel and they finish off the zombies in their backyard.

Despite the television warning against it, Shaun and Ed decide that they have to go rescue Shaun's parents. Barbara tells Shaun that Phillip has been bitten. The two go through several plans, all of them involving killing Philip. Pete has already been bitten, as well, so Shaun and Ed steal his car to take it to Shaun's parents. They recover Shaun's parents and plan to head to The Winchester to wait out the zombie crisis.

They go to get more of their friends to bring with them. They get David, Liz, and Dianne and head to the pub. Philip dies en route.

They make their way to the pub on foot, meeting Yvonne. Once they get into the pub, Shaun and Ed get into an argument, which attracts the zombies. They manage to get inside the pub and barricade themselves in.

Barbara has been bitten and turns into a zombie, forcing Shaun to kill her. The jukebox cranks out a Queen song at one point, attracting the zombies into the building. The Winchester lever-action rifle above the bar, however, turns out to be a real rifle and Shaun uses it to defend the group against the dead. Ed is bitten and Shaun, Liz, and Ed hide out in the basement.

They know it's only a matter of time before the zombies break in, and so Liz and Shaun make sure they have enough bullets left to kill themselves rather than get eaten. Ed volunteers to stay behind and hold them off, however, as he's mortally wounded and Shaun and Liz use an elevator to get back above ground.

Shaun and Liz get ready to go at the zombies again, but soldiers show up and begin massacring the undead.

The zombie apocalypse comes and goes and Shaun and Liz end up together. The zombies have been either killed off or, if they survived, have been used for entertainment and as workers. Ed is shown, zombified, in the shed, playing video games.

A High-End Zom Com

This is one of the zom coms that manages to be good, rather than just a series of in-jokes. The characters are very likeable and Shaun and Ed are world-class slackers, providing plenty of amusement. Ed's solution to Shaun's depression over losing Liz is to get drunk the next day. The two are already getting drunk when Ed suggests it.

Shaun and Ed's friendship dominates the first half of the movie, and despite the fact that Ed is something of a parasite, it's easy enough to see why Shaun likes him. He's fun. Shaun's friends remark that Ed does nothing. Shaun counters that Ed sells marijuana sometimes, to which Pete remarks that Ed only sold weed once, to Shaun, in college. Ed's a loser, to be sure, but he's a good guy.

Despite the fact that this is a comedy, it handles things a bit more realistically than some of the more serious zombie films. The sequence in the backyard of Shaun's house, when he and Ed throw records at the zombies, is one of the funniest, but also feels real. In many zombie movies, the characters go from not knowing what's going on to shooting and bashing in the heads of zombies in a few minutes. Shaun and Ed need a bit more convincing before they're willing to resort to murder.

The humor in this film is more sophisticated than films such as *Return of the Living Dead* and its sequels. The slapstick elements are all very dark and the situation involves several characters dying. If you have a very dark sense of humor, you'll probably love this film.

There are different kinds of zombie comedies out there, and not all of them are for everyone. In addition to what the previous paragraph notes, the characters that die in this film are sometimes quite likeable. It's not a film that presents a group of shallow characters with the understanding that they mostly exist to be killed in some horrible way. Again, it is dark but it's also very, very funny.

Enjoying These Zombies

Some of the best zombie films of the 2000s feature fast zombies. It became apparent as soon as they came onto the scene that simply making them fast and rabid gave zombies an entirely unexplored range of possibilities as antagonists. *Shaun of the Dead*, however, makes a good decision in keeping the zombies slow.

The slow zombies don't rush the characters, which gives plenty of time for dialogue between attacks. The dialogue in this film is one of its strongest elements, so it's a good thing for the film that the zombies are of the slower variety. In fact, in this film, they are really,

really slow. They're slower than Romero's zombies, for the most part. When they present a hazard, it's purely based on them being able to overwhelm their victims with numbers. Other than that, they're easily avoided and killed. In fact, at the end, we find out that they're easily used for slave labor and entertainment, as well.

Some of the best sequences in this film literally make the zombies into background. All around Shaun, there are strange things going on. The culmination occurs when he goes to a store nearby his house the morning the zombie apocalypse has gone into full swing. He doesn't even notice what's going on. Shaun isn't a bad guy at all, but he's not ambitious, and not really engaged with his life. Ed is even worse, and they're both a lot of fun to watch.

Not all zombie comedies are very good. Some zombie horror films already have such strong elements of comedy in them that even making a zombie film an obvious comedy can result in very blocky, silly results. This film, along with others such as *Zombieland*, featured later in this book, manages to offer something more enjoyable than that. Like *Zombieland*, this film is written creatively enough to be enjoyable and to offer an interesting story in a framework that, even by 2004, was already quite well used. This film isn't self-aware like *Return of the Living Dead* or *The Dead Hate the Living!* It's not a bad film that's blissfully unaware of the fact, like *Plan 9 from Outer Space*. This film is written as a comedy set during a zombie apocalypse and it's good in terms of both being funny and being a decent zombie film. It's worth seeing.

Land of the Dead (2005)

Director:

George A. Romero

Starring:

Dennis Hopper

Simon Baker

Asia Argento

Robert Joy

John Leguizamo

Land of the Dead is the fourth film in Romero's series. It follows chronologically after the events depicted in *Day of the Dead*. This film continues the story of humanity's survival after the zombie apocalypse and the evolution of the dead as they continue to take over the Earth.

The Plot

In this film, humanity has begun to rebuild, at least to some degree. A high-rise building serves as the center of a new community, which enjoys the protection of Paul Kaufman, a wealthy businessman. The building is known as Fiddler's Green, but it's only accessible to the rich. For the poor, life is a constant struggle to stay alive as hordes of zombies prowl the ruins of society. Supplies are scarce.

Fiddler's Green has at its disposal a large vehicle named Dead Reckoning. It's outfitted with armor, plenty of weapons, and fireworks. The survivors have figured out that the zombies become entranced by the firework displays and, while the zombies look at the "sky flowers," the humans can operate without interference when retrieving supplies or performing other tasks.

The muscle behind Dead Reckoning is a man named Riley, who's recently given up his command.

It's become apparent, at least to those who have to risk their lives among the undead, that the zombies are evolving. They're becoming smarter over time. The film focuses particularly on one zombie called Big Daddy, who wears a gas station uniform and who seems to have some semblance of memory and certainly a capacity to learn. He seems genuinely distressed when a fellow zombie is slaughtered in front of him.

Civilization isn't quite civilized yet, and Riley goes to a bar and sees a woman being fed to the zombies. He rescues the woman, named Slack, along with the help of Charlie, but it results in their being arrested.

Kaufman was behind Slack being killed. Kaufman and the Fiddler's Green crowd have managed to live the high life, but the people in the city aren't content and are starting to fight back. Their leader is a man named Mulligan.

Cholo, one of the crew on Dead Reckoning, wants to move into Fiddler's Green. He's not allowed to, and, in retaliation, uses Dead Reckoning to threaten the entire high rise. Riley intervenes, and the two seem pitted against one another, until a Kaufman loyalist attacks them both. The two decide not to interfere with one another. Riley wants to head north with Dead Reckoning. Cholo opts to take off on his own.

The zombies begin to invade. They've figured out basic tools. Big Daddy uses a jackhammer to break through the window on Fiddler's Green. A horde floods the building, killing everyone in sight. Kaufmann attempts to flee the building with bags full of money, but is foiled when Big Daddy attacks his car. Big Daddy sticks a gas pump through the windshield, flooding the car and the garage with gasoline.

Cholo comes back and attacks Kaufmann as he attempts to flee. Big Daddy appears at the entrance to the garage and sets the gasoline on fire, killing Kaufmann. Dead Reckoning and its crew head off to Canada. As they're leaving, Riley tells them to shoot off their fireworks. The zombies have evolved to the point that they're no longer hypnotized by them, and Riley doesn't seem inclined to kill them on sight, in any regard.

The Dead Continue to Evolve

Romero's zombies have always shown some indication that they remember their pasts or have some level of intelligence, except in *Night of the Living Dead*. Even in *Dawn of the Dead*, one of the characters who becomes zombified seems to remember where and how the characters had camouflaged their hideout.

In *Day of the Dead*, we see a zombie, having had sufficient contact with a living human, evolve enough to use a firearm and hold a grudge. In this film, Big Daddy is used as a way to show how much zombies really are evolving.

Big Daddy seems horrified and anguished when another zombie is killed in front of him. He also figures out that the rivers that separate the city from the outlying areas can be crossed. It is he who leads the zombies into Fiddler's Green. By the end of the film, he's figured out how fire and accelerants work.

In this film, the humans are the ones who aren't evolving and, oddly enough, they seem more of a threat to one another than anything else. Kaufmann and the Fiddler's Green crowd actually have it very good in the high rise. They have food and supplies and are really quite comfortable. This small group of people control the greatest share of resources, starving out the other people with whom they share the city. It's a not-too-subtle metaphor for class stratification, of course, and that plays into the entire plot.

The dead, on the other hand, seem to just want to survive. They eat people when they can, but people eat other animals and predation isn't necessarily a moral issue. Starving out the majority of people while a select group feasts, however, does have some moral implications and ugliness written into it.

The wealthy get their own in this film, as well. In fact, they seem to get the worst of it and Big Daddy and his shuffling crew seem to understand the wealthy are responsible for killing them off, and go right for the high rise when they get to town.

The film does have a message underneath it all and it's not too hard to figure out. It's not heavy-handed about it, however, and it manages to stay enjoyable throughout.

The Gore

There is plenty of zombie gore here, particularly during the sequence where the living dead descend upon the high rise. There are some very nasty endings to enjoy in this film. Romero generally doesn't disappoint in this regard, and he doesn't in this film, either.

Interestingly, however, the way the zombies are portrayed means that there's more focus on how they die. Instead of just watching characters make headshots or take zombies apart in other creative ways, these zombies are rather sympathetic. There are some interesting issues raised, as well.

For instance, plenty of zombie films add to the overall gruesomeness by having parts of the zombies remain living after being removed from the main body. The head, for instance, may still try to bite whatever's in front of it or, at least, will continue to look around after it's severed. In this film, one of Big Daddy's zombie friends is killed in this way and Big Daddy finishes him off by crushing his decapitated head. He seems to realize what a hell it would be to live on as a decapitated head and puts the other zombie out of its misery.

This makes the zombies more sympathetic and, in fact, makes the whole back-from-the-grave concept even more disturbing.

Enjoying These Zombies

This is a decent film all around and is worth watching. It's also part of Romero's series of zombie films, of course, and that means that it's a must-see for any serious fan.

This continues on what started in *Day of the Dead* quite nicely. Because it was made much later, however, some things are a bit off.

For instance, Dead Reckoning has very sophisticated weaponry and computer systems, but *Day of the Dead* takes place in a much less technologically advanced world. Somehow, humans continued to develop their technology, even though most of the infrastructure to do that must be gone.

It does follow logically with what goes on in *Day of the Dead* from a social point of view, and does so quite nicely. In *Day of the Dead*, the lead scientist had become such an exaggeration of himself that he was doing experiments that were ethically out of bounds. The soldiers had become authoritarian, homicidal cartoons of a sort, ranting and raving and threatening anyone and everyone who wasn't a soldier.

In this film, the wealthy have literally put themselves up in a fortified castle and left anyone not among them to starve—or worse—out in the slums around their castle. No one is allowed in who isn't a member, and working one's way into Fiddler's Green is a dream that's used to sucker the poor, like Cholo, into serving the interests of the rich. When the poor are no longer useful, they're discarded and most certainly not let into the high rise themselves. They're so over the top in their notions of entitlement that it's impossible to like them. They make fine villains, as does Kaufman, the worst of the lot.

Those outside the high rise take all the risks and go up against the dead, even though they don't reap all the benefits of their work. The dead themselves don't actually go after the slums when they raid the high rise. The zombies seem to have figured out that the folks in the high rise are just pitting the poor against the dead and benefitting from the entire bloody enterprise. In the end, everyone rebels, even the zombies.

This film definitely has its moments. It's not nearly as important in the overall history of zombie films as are *Night of the Living Dead* or *Dawn of the Dead*. In fact, films such as the remake of *Dawn of the Dead* and *28 Days Later* have likely had more impact on the image of zombies in modern culture. It is, however, an interesting film among Romero's canon and he knows how to make a good zombie story come together. The evolution of the dead is an interesting premise to follow through the entirety of the films and he does a good job of further developing it here.

Fido (2006)

Director:

Andrew Currie

Starring:

Carrie-Anne Moss

Dylan Baker

Billy Connolly

K'Sun Ray

Fido is a zom com produced in Canada that sets the action in a sort of alternate universe where *Leave It to Beaver* meets *Day of the Dead*. The film has a bit of gore here and there but, for the most part, the juxtaposition of a deadly zombie, a cute kid and the suburban, idyllic family of the 1950s carries the film.

The Plot

This film takes the zombie origin story to its Romero roots, with the zombies having risen up from the grave due to radiation from space. After the Zombie Wars had passed, the plague is still in effect, but the remaining humans have learned how to deal with the dead rising from their graves. They either dispatch the zombies in the traditional ways—cut their head off or burn them—or they enslave them for cheap labor and as pets of a sort.

The action takes place in the town of Willard. The main characters are Timmy, the young boy, and his parents, Helen and Bill. Helen is gentle and kind most of the time. Bill hates zombies, due to having trauma from having fought off the zombies during the initial outbreak.

Timmy has a strong bond with his zombie Fido, who is controlled via a collar provided by the Zomcon company. The Zomcon company provides zombie slaves and keeps the community safe from an invasion of the creatures.

Fido gets loose one day and attacks an annoying neighbor, killing her. Timmy covers up the crime, but the neighbor manages to spread the plague a bit, which is contained. Later, two other neighborhood boys who don't care much for Timmy are blamed for the entire incident.

The boys catch Timmy and Fido and tie them to trees. One of the boys idiotically destroys Fido's collar, ending any means of keeping him under control. Fido attacks the boys and turns them into zombies, but runs back to find Helen so that she can rescue Timmy. As the two are driving back to get Timmy, Helen notices that Fido's collar is broken but that he's not attacking. The zombie has apparently bonded with them.

They find Timmy and save him, while Helen casually shoots the two young zombie boys. After they return home, however, Fido's eating of the neighbor catches up with him and he is taken away. He's supposed to be destroyed, but Zomcon merely puts him to work.

A former security officer at Zomcon, who is now in love with a zombie, helps Timmy to get Fido back. Mr. Bottoms, the current chief of security, catches them, and Fido saves Timmy from Mr. Bottoms, but not before Timmy's dad, Bill, is killed by the security chief.

The whole thing is covered up and Bill is decapitated to prevent him from turning into a zombie. Fido moves in with Timmy and his family and becomes one of them.

Not Bad

While not as dark or funny as *Shaun of the Dead*, *Fido* is certainly enjoyable enough. Fido's predicament is a bit reminiscent of that of the creature in *Bride of Frankenstein*, where he's not bad at all but people treat him like a monster just because of what he is. He can't really help eating the occasional person, but he doesn't do it out of a desire to kill anything in his path, as most film zombies do.

In some scenes, Fido is rather like Lassie in the old serials, coming to warn Helen that Timmy is in trouble and needs help. He's really quite sweet, though nothing of substance is revealed about him, where he came from, or who he was before becoming a zombie. This film is very light, despite the subject matter, and it doesn't delve too deeply into those waters.

K'Sun Ray plays Timmy and he's very good in the role, looking and sounding like just about every kid on every family-friendly sitcom from the 1950s and 1960s. He's very attached to Fido and dreads anything bad happening to him. Essentially, it's a boy-and-his-dog story, except the dog in this case happens to be an undead creature that was risen from the grave by space radiation. The film's style, with its perfect suburbs and clean and neat people, provides a great atmosphere for the humor that's being used and, for the most part, it works.

What works very well is that the plot is really something right out of one of those old sitcoms, except for the murders and zombie shootings. Everyone gets to redeem themselves at the end—if they've shown any substantial flaws—and the film has a weird, but happy, ending.

Enjoying These Zombies

This is a zom com, but it never really strays into the dark territory that other films of this type tend to explore. It's fun, not at all serious, and manages to do a good job of taking what could be a quickly worn-out joke and making it work.

The sense of safety and wonder that ran through those old sitcoms, oddly enough, is very much on display. In the end, the film is more about accepting zombies for who they are and recognizing that, apparently, they have feelings, too.

The zombies themselves aren't particularly interesting, though it seems that's intentional. They're radiation zombies that move slowly, but, unlike the zombies in most horror films, seem to be easily controlled and rather sweet, at least in some cases. The former security chief at Zomcon even has a zombie girlfriend, and, in the end, Timmy appears to have a sort of zombie stepfather.

The film might be tedious for those who really like the dark humor that defines the best of zombie comedies, but look a little deeper and you'll see that it's there. This film is at its best when it delves into satire, such as when one of the main characters becomes a much better father after he's been zombified and the nastiness has been taken out of his personality. Helen is shown having genuine affection for Fido and, in fact, he actually seems to be closer to Timmy than Timmy's own dad is. Timmy's dad has a hatred for zombies that makes him unpleasant at times, but Fido is quite fun to spend time with, it seems.

The best thing about this film is that it demonstrates that, with good writing and creativity, people can still make zombie films that are original and entertaining. Thus far, films like this seem to indicate that, at least as of yet, the zombie storyline hasn't devolved into the dead-end, boring tropes it did for a while in the 1980s and 1990s, and that there's still enough interest among the talented writers out there to make these films work.

[Rec](2007)

Director:

Jaume Balaguero

Paco Plaza

Starring:

Manuela Velasco

Ferran Terraza

Jorge-Yamam Serrano

Pablo Rosso

[Rec] is a Spanish film that takes us through a zombie outbreak in an interesting and effective way. It uses the first-person style of shooting, with the film set up as having been made by a news crew as they follow a group of firefighters on their nightly rounds. Things go seriously awry.

The Plot

Angela Vidal and Pablo, her cameraman, work for a show called *While You're Sleeping*. The documentary series runs at night, and, on this particular night, they've decided to follow a group of firefighters in Barcelona. They settle in for the night shift with the fire crew and seem disappointed to find out, both from the men and from their own unfolding experiences, that the night shift as a firefighter is generally pretty dull.

The firefighters give the group a tour of their station and show off their equipment, but the night is uneventful. Finally, a call comes in, but it seems minor. It's regarding a woman who is apparently trapped in her own apartment.

The crew and some of the firefighters take off to render assistance. When they get there, the police have already arrived and are resistant to having the camera crew with them. However, Angela maintains that she has permission to be there.

The police break into the woman's apartment and go in to help. When they approach her, she attacks them, viciously biting the ranking police officer. The others manage to fight her off, but, outside the lobby of the apartment building, the military has arrived. The film crew, police officers, fire crew, and residents in the apartment building are warned to stay away from the doors and a plastic quarantine tent is dropped over the building.

The woman kills one of the firefighters and tosses him down the stairs. The rest of the police and firefighters go up to deal with her and the camera crew follows. The woman goes after the men again, but they shoot her, apparently killing her.

Tension rises between the film crew and the police officer, who wants them to stop filming. One of the residents' daughter, Jennifer, is sick. She's waiting for her husband to return with medicine. She says that Jennifer has tonsillitis. Jennifer talks about how her dog Max is also sick and at the vet when Angela interviews her.

Finally, someone from the outside comes in to render assistance. A health inspector enters the building wearing a hazmat suit. He goes to help the people who have been bitten, curiously insisting that they be handcuffed to the gurneys they're lying on, in a workshop in the back of the apartment building. It's not a mystery for long, however, as the people who were bitten begin attacking anyone close enough to bite. Angela and Pablo film the action through a window.

The crew finally corners the health inspector and demands answers. He reveals that the disease that's going around was first discovered at a veterinarian's office, when a dog that was brought in with a strange illness. The dog went into a coma, came out, and then started attacking anything and everything it could. The dog, of course, is Jennifer's dog, Max.

Jennifer turns, bites her mother in the face and takes off up the stairs while everyone is stunned. The police handcuff her mother to the staircase—the disease spreads by bites—and take off after Jennifer, followed by the film crew and the remaining firefighter.

The firefighter and the police officer find Jennifer and try to recover her, but she bites the police officer in the process. The infected that the health inspector was trying to treat have started pushing their way into the apartment building's lobby from the workshop. They cannot stop the infected, so Pablo and one of the residents, Manu, run up the stairs to get away, leaving Jennifer's mother to be eaten.

They make it to Manu's apartment, where he tells them that there is a way out of the building. There is a key in the apartment manager's quarters to an exit in the workshop that they can use to get out via the sewers, avoiding the quarantine.

The health inspector becomes infected in the meantime. They abandon him and head to the apartment manager's apartment.

They get the keys, but the undead are coming. The firefighter is killed and, with only Angela and Pablo left, they cannot make it through the infected to get to the workshop, so they take shelter in the penthouse.

The penthouse is full of religious icons and press clippings, detailing cases of demonic possession. They focus on one girl who was a victim of sexual abuse by priests. The resident of the penthouse had worked for the Vatican and was trying to cure the girl.

Interestingly, the possession is linked to the zombie plague. The girl was abandoned to die by the resident of the apartment, left in a sealed room.

Pablo and Angela continue to explore the house. When Pablo uses the camera to see what's in an attic without sticking his head in it, the light on the camera is broken. He switches to night vision mode, reducing the screen to the characteristic dark greens and grays.

Soon enough, they find where the girl that the resident was working on was kept. The girl is still alive, but is starved down to a skeleton. She finds and kills Pablo. Angela picks up the camera but loses her balance, falling down. The last shot we see is of her being dragged back from the frame into the dark.

Overused Idea but Done Well

There are many films out there, particularly horror films, which use the first-person camera to add tension to the film. *Paranormal Activity*, *Diary of the Dead*, and *V/H/S* are only a few of them. Sometimes it works, sometimes it doesn't, but in this film, it does.

This film really doesn't make a gimmick out of the perspective. It's just a natural way to tell the story, given the circumstances under which it occurs. The film crew following the fire department is great motivation to have a camera there during the outbreak of the zombie apocalypse, and it works very well.

The camera work manages to capture the chaos of the moment, but doesn't get to the motion sickness-inducing extremes seen in other films that use this style. The presumption that the man operating the camera is a professional allows for steady shots that are framed well and that follow the action—at least until things explode—and that make it much easier to follow what's going on in this film than in many others of its type.

The Possession Connection

The scenes before the finale are a nice touch and they actually serve to introduce a new monster into a film that could have been effectively finished with just the zombies. The idea that the Vatican investigator would be treating zombification as a spiritual problem is also interesting. The cruelty implied by leaving the girl behind to starve is disturbing but, then again, the girl herself seems to be a walking nightmare of the same caliber as Samara from *The Ring*.

She's very, very creepy and the night vision does a lot to bring that out.

The sparing use of night vision also adds a particular sense of menace to the final scenes of the film.

Enjoying These Zombies

[Rec] does a great job of showing chaos on-screen without making it unintelligible. There are only a few sets to deal with and the ones that are introduced are shown enough to give the viewer some sense of where things are. This isn't one of those first-person films where the characters start running and the camera shakes so much that you have no idea where they are, where they're headed, or what's in front or behind them. *[Rec]* does an excellent job of giving the audience some sense of the environment the action is taking place in and doesn't overuse the frantic camera trope.

The zombies are very effective. They're not undead. They go into a coma and, when they wake up; they're very aggressive and immediately attack anything in front of them. It's a definite invocation of a rabies-type disease. The ending, however, implies that it may have some supernatural overtones as well, and that makes it really quite interesting. It keeps it from becoming yet another film about the zombification process being all plague and nothing supernatural, at any rate.

This film is in Spanish, so those who don't speak it will definitely need a subtitled copy. This film won several awards and was nominated for many others.. It's among the better zombie films of the last 10 years, to be certain.

28 Weeks Later (2007)

Director:
Juan Carlos Fresnadillo

Starring:

Robert Carlyle

Rose Byrne

Jeremy Renner

Catherine McCormack

Harold Perrineau

The sequel to *28 Days Later*, this film completely abandons the original characters and tells a story set in the same universe but with very different players and different stakes. It's just as dark as the original and, once it gets going, just as violent and intense. It has good reviews overall and provides a solid continuation of the story of the Rage virus and how it devastated the UK.

The Plot

The story starts out in the same period as the original. Alice, Don, and others have found shelter in a remote cottage, but the infected are not far behind. After cooking canned food for dinner, the survivors hear a knock at the door. A young boy is on the run and seeks shelter with them, which they offer. The infected are hot on his heels, however, and they soon overwhelm the cottage.

Don, Alice and the boy try to flee upstairs but get separated. Alice pleads with Don for help, but seeing that there's nothing he can do, he dives out a window and takes off on his own. He makes it to a friend who has a motorboat and barely manages to get away from the

Rage zombies. They continue to pursue him in the water, with several of them being chopped up by the propeller on the boat.

As was established in the first film, the zombies do starve after a time. The UK is ready for rebuilding, but on a small scale. To provide protection, a NATO-led group of soldiers, mostly Americans, have secured an area of London. After the titular 28 weeks have passed, the NATO force starts bringing in people to repopulate the safe area of the city.

Don has gotten a decent position in the secure area of London. His children, who were abroad studying at the time, return to London to join him, leading the chief medical officer, Levy, to complain that she hadn't been notified that they were bringing in children. As one of Don's children, Andy, goes through screening, Levy notes that he has heterochromia, which is usually an inherited trait. He says that his mother had it, too.

Two military characters are introduced. Sergeant Doyle is a sniper with Delta Force, stationed on a catwalk, and, along with several others of his kind, monitor the situation from above. Flynn is a chief and a helicopter pilot, and one of Doyle's close friends.

Don and his children bond with one another. He tells them what happened to his mother and how the military gave him shelter until the Rage zombies all died off. Andy has nightmares about forgetting his mother. They decide to sneak away from the guarded area to get a picture of her.

Doyle sees the children leave and sends a patrol after them. Their mother is discovered alive, but barely aware of her surroundings. She's taken into quarantine.

Under examination, it's discovered that Alice is a carrier of the Rage virus, but some sort of abnormality in her system prevents her from becoming symptomatic. She does show the characteristic changes in her eyes, however, which are slightly red.

Don finds out that his wife is alive and sneaks in to see her. He apologizes to her for abandoning her and seems genuinely anguished. She seems to forgive him and the two kiss. Within seconds, Don starts to show signs of the Rage infection. He turns into a Rage zombie and tears Alice apart before going after others in the facility.

The safe zone has safety protocols and they immediately go into effect. The security situation is referred to as Code Red. First, the military tries to protect the civilians by taking them to safe areas and sealing them in. Unfortunately, Don manages to get into one of these rooms and attacks, spreading the Rage virus within minutes.

Levy realizes that Don and Alice's children, Andy and Tammy, could have the same abnormality their mother had, making them possible sources of a vaccine or cure for the zombie plague. She manages to save them from the containment area.

The snipers on the catwalks initially try to gun down the infected, but have trouble picking them out from the healthy civilians. Panic has taken over the safe zone and crowds of people run underneath them. Soon enough, an order is issued: anything on the ground is a valid target, even civilians. Doyle cannot go along with this and manages to get to Levy, Tammy, and Andy.

Doyle resolves to help the children escape. Along with some other survivors, they succeed in getting out of the safe zone. The military firebombs the entire area, but it's not effective and many of the infected survive, continuing the spread of the plague.

Doyle radios his friend, Flynn, and asks for an extraction. While they wait for Flynn, Levy explains that the children could hold the key to curing the plague and, therefore, their lives are worth more than hers or Doyle's. Doyle understands fully.

Flynn shows up but doesn't want to take the children with him, insisting that only Doyle and Flynn go. Doyle tries to explain the situation but one of the men with them jumps on the landing gear of the helicopter. Flynn takes off, trying to shake him loose. He then takes the helicopter and uses the blades to massacre the infected that are chasing after Doyle, Levy, and the children.

Flynn radios Doyle again and tells him to meet him at Wembley Stadium for an extraction. He still refuses to take the civilians, but Doyle is now committed to getting the children to safety.

The group head through the city, but the military releases nerve gas to kill off the remaining infected. The group hides out in a car, waiting for the gas to dissipate. The infected soon attack and Levy cannot get the car to start. Seeing that military personnel with flamethrowers are making their way down the street, Doyle tells Levy to pop the clutch and exits the car so they can push start it. As he pushes the car and they get underway, the military personnel catch up to him and incinerate him with their flamethrowers.

Levy and the children make their way through the city, being chased by a helicopter along the way. They manage to get into the subway and abandon the car. Don shows up again and kills Levy. Andy also gets bitten, and Tammy kills her father to protect Andy. Andy shows no symptoms of infection other than having the discolored eyes.

Flynn meets the children at the stadium. Doyle tells him to get the children across the English Channel and he agrees, taking them out of the infected area.

The story picks up 28 days later. The helicopter is shown, but there's no one left in it. A horde of infected are rampaging through the streets, which are revealed to be Parisian streets as the film closes. The infection has spread outside the UK.

A Solid Sequel

It's hard to live up to a film like *28 Days Later*, but, for the most part, this film does. The plot moves more slowly than in the original, particularly during the portion where the characters are being established and where the second and third acts are being set up.

The film has the same quick, violent action as the first, though there's less of a sense of confusion present. In the first film, particularly during Jim's initial encounters with the zombies, no one knew exactly what was going on or what had caused it. In this film, the characters clearly know what they're running from and how high the stakes are.

The plague hasn't changed much from the first film to this one, which is a strength. This helps to avoid situations like what happened with the *Aliens* franchise, where the incubation period for the aliens went from more than a day to around 30 seconds. In this film, keeping the virus consistent makes it seem more real. The infected may have starved to death, but the virus lived on in asymptomatic carriers, those who have the virus but who don't suffer from the symptoms that affect others.

This plot development, of course, is not without precedent. There are people out there who can, and who have, carried contagious diseases and who spread them to others without coming down with the fatal symptoms themselves. The most famous is Typhoid Mary, who managed to spread her namesake disease to horrible effect before she was identified and stopped by the authorities. Frighteningly, and in another parallel with this film, many of the carriers don't even know they have Rage. This is exactly what happens to Andy at the end of the film. While saving the children and getting them out of the UK may have led to the creation of a vaccine had they not been infected, Andy basically becomes an open Petri dish when he's bitten by his father. He apparently distributes the contagion in France once he gets there.

This film plays out well in terms of giving the audience a sequel that takes the zombie plague just as seriously as the first, and also manages to do so without becoming silly or resorting to huge changes in the plot to keep it all interesting. There's one other area where this film performs well, also, and it's one of the most unpleasant aspects of the first film.

Hard Choices

If you were Andy, Tammy, or Levy, Doyle is exactly the type of solider that you'd want protecting you. He's a top-notch sniper, as is firmly established in the scene where he takes out a less competent shooter when he's helping Levy and the children escape. He notes that the sniper takes more than one shot to hit the mirror Doyle uses to spot him. When he tries to persuade a survivor to run out into the sniper's area of coverage, Doyle assures the man that the other sniper will miss, and Doyle won't. Doyle makes good on that prediction.

When the helicopter shows up, Flynn is set up as somewhat of a bad guy, refusing to take the children on the helicopter. As in the first film, we're presented with a character who does something that seems unfair and even murderous, but is Flynn really the bad guy here? Are Levy and Doyle really good guys for abandoning their posts and defying orders to help the children escape?

If Levy had managed to get Andy and Tammy out of the nation without them coming into contact with the infected, it could have led to a breakthrough in the containment or even curing of Rage. However, the military had determined that the situation was far too out-of-control to risk letting anyone leave the containment area. As brutal as that may seem, it's hard to argue in that regard.

The infection spreads in seconds and the infected are mixed in with the uninfected at the outset of the outbreak. Even the military personnel start getting overwhelmed and infected. This disease spreads through a population in minutes and is almost impossible to contain once it gets going.

While Doyle's orders were certainly horrific in their implications, they weren't unreasonable. Letting Rage get out of London carries the implication that civilization could be wiped out in days, if not faster. Gunning down uninfected civilians is brutal, to be sure, but it's better than having the entire world infected and losing the species, possibly the entire planet, in the end. What Doyle did was noble and certainly self-sacrificing, but he also made a decision to defy a perfectly sensible order.

In many films, there are scenes where military characters begin complaining that they're doing something that they didn't sign up for. Of course, when one signs up, there's the implication—and obligation—that they're signing up to do whatever they're told to do. Doyle may have had sympathetic reasons for not wanting to shoot civilians, but he certainly didn't have any logical reasons.

Flynn may have seemed uncaring or even cruel to want to leave the children behind, but his decision in this regard made perfect sense and would likely have spared the world from the infection. In both of these films, characters have to make hard choices and, in the end, it's not readily apparent who the good guy is and who the bad guy is. In the first film, for instance, Major West has a zombie chained in the backyard so he can determine how long it takes them to starve out, which he believes will be the end of the plague. It seems cruel, but, at the outset of *28 Weeks Later*, we find out that West was right. The UK had to wait for the zombies to starve to death before they could start repopulating, and, as brutal as West's method of research was, he was on the right track.

In just about every zombie film, there's a part where one of the main characters or, at least, one of the secondary characters, gets infected and has to be dispatched by their allies for the good of everyone else. In the *28 Days Later* films, this choice is amplified in terms of its urgency. Most films allow the characters to wait for a stricken ally to succumb to the disease and then to kill off their risen corpse. In this film, it's more like shooting a rabid dog, where the infected character is alive and, if there was some sort of cure, they could probably be helped. This is part of the darkness in both of these films and it's done very effectively. The fact that these films both have good actors giving excellent performances only helps make them harder to watch at times.

Enjoying These Zombies

28 Weeks Later manages to pull off quite a cinematic feat. It shows us an antagonist character—both the Rage virus and the zombies it creates—that we're already familiar with and manages to keep them scary enough to drive the plot along. In many films, once the audience and the characters understand the nature of the horror, it loses a lot of its punch. Not so in this film. The infected are just as scary as they were in its predecessor.

In this film, we also see a nice portrayal of how the lines between right and wrong start to blur in a situation like the Rage virus infections. Normally, people have a nice delineation between the two that suits the situations they experience in their everyday lives. Because the situation in these films is so far outside of the norm, it's impossible to tell, sometimes, who's really right and wrong. The military, when they start gunning down anything that moves, firebombing and nerve-gassing London, seem like antagonists on the outside, but it's easy to understand why they're taking those measures. In fact, the only outright mistake they make is in repopulating London too soon, when the virus is still out there.

The military isn't evil in this film, but whoever decided that Rage was a thing of the past was certainly guilty of being arrogant.

The characters in this film, even Don, have some moral murkiness, as well. Don abandons his wife, but it's not clear what he really could have done to save her. The zombies were banging at the door, they were all over the house and, as we've seen already in this series, they're very hard to fight off. One bite or one stray bit of blood in the eye or mouth and you're infected. The only real defense is to run or to kill them from a distance with a firearm.

Andy and Tammy aren't good or bad, but they don't understand what's going on with them either, to everyone's peril. Andy and Tammy just want to get out of the UK—who wouldn't, in this film?—and end up spreading the contagion because of that. If only Flynn had followed his orders.

This film shows how human weakness and, even more, traits that people generally regard as strengths—loyalty, mercy, fairness—can become fatal liabilities in certain situations. When there's a fast-moving plague on the loose and when its victims can spread it in seconds, it's really not a good time to be nostalgic. To paraphrase Mark Helprin in *A Solider of the Great War*, guilt has no place on a farm or in war. The same seems to hold true here. When the infected are intermingled with the healthy, and when they're both tangled up in a chaotic riot, your best bet is to just follow orders, take all of them down and save the entire world in the process.

28 Weeks Later is among the rare sequels out there that lives up to its predecessor. It offers a fresh story, a novel one at that, and keeps the zombie apocalypse form becoming so familiar that it loses all its power to scare. This film isn't a pleasant one and the ending certainly has a down note to it, but it's hard to imagine that it could have turned out any other way. This is one of the films featured in this book that is definitely worth seeing and that serious film fans will likely very much enjoy. It's worth enduring the slower parts at the beginning.

Diary of the Dead (2007)

Director:

George A. Romero

Starring:

Josh Close

Michelle Morgan

Shawn Roberts

Amy Lalonde

Joe Dinicol

George A. Romero returned to the world of the living dead in 2007 with this found-footage-style film. It doesn't fit in neatly with the others in his series, but it is a part of the same overarching mythology. This film is done in a different style to the others, though it has many of the hallmarks that have come to define Romero's zombie films.

The Plot

This film doesn't follow the narrative established by the other films in Romero's *Dead* franchise. It does, however, follow the popular convention of films seen from the first-person documentary view. This means that the entire film is shot as if the viewer is watching someone experience the dead rising while making video of the entire thing.

First, we see news reporters covering a murder-suicide. The crime involves a man who shot his wife and son and then took his own life.

As the reporters record their stories, we see the dead starting to rise from the gurneys, with one of them tearing out the throat of a medic.

From there, a narrator, Debra, gives us an overview of what happened. The news footage we saw was never broadcast, implying a cover up.

The action cuts to a woman being chased through the woods. The filming stops and we realize that it's a film set and a group of students and an advisor are working on a horror film. While they're working, news comes in that civil disturbances are cropping up all over. People are being murdered and riots are breaking out, prompting the crew to leave their shoot to see what's going on and to make contact with loved ones.

It becomes clear that there's more to what's happening than standard rioting and murder. As the group heads back to their families, they encounter the risen dead. Mary cannot handle it and tries to shoot herself. When they take her in for assistance, they find the hospital is teeming with zombies. They have weapons, and Maxwell does some impressive bow-and-arrow work, but they have to flee after the zombies overwhelm them and infect some of the cast members.

They get away, but the RV they're in breaks down. An Amish man helps them out. He can't hear and uses a blackboard to communicate. The man, however, ends up getting bitten.

They encounter some other survivors, some of whom are soldiers. Debra finds out her family avoided the attacks and are going back home. The group decides to head to Debra's house to meet them.

By the time they get there, Debra's family has turned and are eating one another. They run into more soldiers, but these soldiers are taking advantage of the chaos by robbing people.

The group makes its way to the home of one of the students, Ridley. By that time, everyone there has been wiped out. Ridley is also zombified and kills Elliot. Jason helps Tracey to get away. She drives off and Jason continues to shoot footage of what's going on. Ridley bites him, but Debra kills him and Maxwell kills Ridley.

The estate is overrun by zombies, but Debra manages to wait it out in the panic room. At the end of the film, over footage of hunters using the living dead for target practice, she wonders whether humanity should be saved.

Similar, but Different

This film is technically a part of the universe that Romero brought into existence with *Night of the Living Dead*. It is, however, much different. This is partially because of its shooting style and partially because of how far removed it is in time from the original film. Like *Night of the Living Dead*, this movie has plenty of messages in it, but they are very different from the ones in that film, as well.

In *Night of the Living Dead*, the media serves as a sort of indicator of society collapsing. The newscasts become more desperate; no one knows what's going on or why—at least at first—and there's widespread panic. In *Dawn of the Dead*, the end of media transmissions signals the worst.

In this film, which is a product of today, the characters themselves are the media, mainly Jason, who keep shooting anything and everything that's going on. Essentially, he's a character who assists his group by documenting everything they do, which he'll presumably someday release as a documentary or, at least, upload to YouTube, one imagines.

Throughout this film, there's the implication that the media can't be trusted. The only reliable information that the characters get comes from bloggers on the Internet. Jason is, of course, a part of that world in his incessant filming of events as they unfold. Romero has said in interviews that he was critiquing both the way that people are seduced into believing that they should be the media, and the way that the internet allows opinions that might not be reasonable or worthwhile to masquerade as fact. There is a lot of that message to chew on in this film.

Jason keeps the camera rolling no matter what. He seems to believe that he's really doing a service by keeping it on, even though his friends could certainly use any help he'd be able to give if he put the camera down.

In Romero's other *Dead* films, there is plenty of social commentary on everything from consumerism to the perils of stratifying society. In this film, the critique is aimed at the viewer. How information is gathered, interpreted and presented are all vital components in people understanding the world around them. While Jason seems to think he's getting useful information, he's really just recording chaos and confusion that offers plenty of terror but no real information.

There's a very interesting parallel between this film and *Night of the Living Dead.* They're both low-budget films where Romero was free to do, essentially, anything he wanted. *Diary of the Dead* is shot on digital cameras, but the shooting is good enough that it's not at all distracting.

In the interview linked above, Romero also mentions that he doesn't consider this film to be in the found-footage genre. Rather, it's a finished documentary made by some of the students depicted in the film. This is why it comes off as a finished piece rather than as just video being shown as it was found. There are some similarities to the found-film genre, and of course, to the film that defines it, *The Blair Witch Project*. However, *Diary of the Dead* does have a different feel throughout that makes it seem more polished. It has far less of the jerky, nausea-inducing camerawork, to be sure.

Enjoying These Zombies

Anything by George Romero is worth seeing for serious zombie fans, even his films that don't live up to his otherwise great reputation. This film offers something quite a bit different from his other films, however, and it's apparent from the start.

The introduction scene, with the corpses getting up off the hospital gurney, has some of the same feel that *Night of the Living Dead* had. It feels like the documentary it's supposed to be. While *Night of the Living Dead* was not shot in this way, it did have that feel quite often, with its grainy film, realistic-looking and sparse sets, and the reactions of the characters to a type of monster they'd never heard of and didn't know how to deal with.

Diary of the Dead has some other very Romero-esque touches throughout that make it clear that it's part of his overall series. We have corrupted soldiers taking advantage of those weaker than themselves, mass murder, rioting and wide-spread confusion. We also have characters who are not really prepared to deal with what they're being presented with, and who have to do their best to survive in spite of that. In essence, we have a Romero zombie flick in every regard.

The big difference is the documentary shooting style, and it does work. The fact that they didn't go pure found-footage style with this film is an asset. It makes it easier to watch and, considering that zombie films and found-footage films are both flooding the horror market at present, it made sense to avoid that cliché. What is possibly most enjoyable about this film is that, decades after he put out *Night of the Living Dead*, George Romero once again managed to take a very small budget, minimal resources and a fast shooting schedule and turn around a great zombie thriller. It's a nice twist on the *Night of the Living Dead* narrative and works quite well.

I Am Legend (2007)

Director:

Francis Lawrence

Starring:

Will Smith

Alice Braga

Dash Mihok

I Am Legend is based on the 1945 Richard Matheson novel by the same title, the same book that provided the source material for the film *The Last Man on Earth*. The film takes a very different tact than *The Last Man on Earth*, however. Given that it's a modern film, it's not surprising that the tone is much darker, but the story is also quite different.

The Plot

In *I Am Legend*, a cure for one of the world's most feared diseases unleashes something far more dangerous.

The story starts in 2009. The measles virus has been engineered into a cure for cancer. The treatment has been very successful but, after a time, it takes a horrible turn. The people given the cure start turning into this film's version of zombies. They combine the vampiric characteristics of the creatures in *The Last Man on Earth* with a great deal of speed and intelligence. They are extremely aggressive. They are also vulnerable to sunlight, which makes it safe to go out in the day. They are called Darkseekers.

The disease spreads quickly through the population. Some people were immune, but were wiped out by those who turned. As far as

Robert Neville, a virologist and Army Lieutenant Colonel knows, he may be the last person alive who hasn't been infected.

It's been three years since the outbreak and Neville is still in New York City, where he remained after a military quarantine was put into effect. His family was killed during the evacuation and, for years, he's been using his own immunity as the basis for research into a possible cure or vaccine. He experiments on animals to test his work and, when necessary, collects Darkseekers to experiment on as well.

The virus only affected humans and domestic animals, so Neville is able to sustain himself on wild game, and on food that he finds and a considerable stash of reserves he's shown to have in his apartment. He has electricity at his house and a dog, Sam, who is his companion.

Despite the fact that he appears to be the last person left, he has a recorded message that plays over the radio every day. He waits at a dock every day at midday for 30 minutes to see if anyone shows up. He always makes it home before dusk, which prevents the Darkseekers from following him and finding out where he lives.

Neville is showing signs that he's cracking, despite the fact that he manages to maintain a routine. He talks to mannequins that he arranges as if they were people going about their business. He's exhausted at times and watches recordings of news broadcasts that he made before the world fell apart.

One day, while he's involved in an argument with one of the mannequins, he gets caught in a trap and ends up suspended high above the street. Sam waits for him and, before long, it's dark enough for the Darkseekers to come out. Sam gets bitten by a dog infected with the virus, but survives. When Neville brings him home, however, he starts to turn into one of the creatures and Neville is forced to kill the dog, the only friend he had left.

Neville appears to fall apart after this and becomes nearly suicidal in his rage. He almost gets himself killed, but survives due to the intervention of Anna, who drives him to safety. She has a young son, Ethan, and the two of them seem to share Neville's immunity to the virus.

Neville insists that they drive until dawn, as the Darkseekers will figure out where he lives if they don't. The next morning, he awakes to find Ethan watching *Shrek* and Anna cooking them all breakfast. Neville, distraught and not having spoken to another human being in years, has a hard time dealing with the two at first, having explosive bursts of anger.

Anna and her son are going to a survivor camp, which they believe is still operating in Vermont. Neville doesn't believe that there's anyone left, but Anna believes that a higher power has been directing her actions.

The Darkseekers find where Neville has been hiding all these years and attack his house, due to Anna not knowing how to keep them from smelling her trail. The final confrontation occurs in Neville's laboratory. The Darkseekers manage to overwhelm the entire house and it's inevitable that they're all going to die.

At the last moment, Neville realizes that the cure he's been working on may actually be effective. He takes a sample of the Darkseekers' blood and gives it to Anna. To ensure that the two get out alive, he ushers them out a chute and then turns on the Darkseekers. He sets off a grenade, killing the Darkseekers, but also killing himself.

Anna and her son make it to the survivor camp and give the personnel the sample of blood. From the ending narration, one can presume that a cure is found later on, based on Neville's work.

A Worthy Successor

Vincent Price's movies oftentimes don't get much credit for being as good as some of them were in spite of the fact that some of them were very low-budget affairs. *The Last Man on Earth*, however, was a decent film. *I Am Legend* was obviously made on a much larger budget, but is similar in some ways.

In *The Last Man on Earth*, the zombies were actually vampires, but they really did behave like zombies. *I Am Legend* manages to have a lot in common with modern zombie films, but the Darkseekers are very vampire-like. The Darkseekers are fast and, in addition to being hungry, seem genuinely hateful toward their prey.

Vampires have been domesticated over the years, going from very sexualized, lethal threats, to centenarian high school vegetarians who date teenage girls. These vampires are feral.

The Last Man on Earth is a dark film. *I Am Legend* is surprisingly dark as well. The world is very bleak and the ending certainly is not happy.

Enjoying These Zombies

These zombies are fast, enraged, and seemingly fearless. They're held back by the sun, but not by much else. They swarm like slow zombies, but they tear at any structure, vehicle or person in their path with a great deal more purpose. They can be on you in seconds.

These creatures aren't really zombies, in the strictest sense. They're vampiric, and, to some degree, almost lycanthropic, as well. They attack like a pack of wolves and they have a leader.

This film can stand well on its own, but watching *The Last Man on Earth* as well will likely give one a greater appreciation of it. The two films are connected by a storyline that melds vampires and zombies with the aforementioned werewolf-like qualities, creating a separate universe of sorts. Like zombie films, the creatures in the older film were slower, more dimwitted, and far less dangerous. Like many stories told on film, this one has been told and retold and adapted to the times it was made it. The story still works and it's worth watching.

Survival of the Dead (2009)

Director:

George A. Romero

Starring:

Alan Van Sprang

Kenneth Welsh

Kathleen Munroe

Devon Bostick

Athena Karkanis

Here we have the final installment—to date—in Romero's *Dead* series. It takes the action to an island located off the coast of Delaware. Like Romero's other films in this series, it is rife with social commentary and commentary on the human condition. It's generally considered the weakest entry in the series, but it does have its moments.

The Plot

Survival of the Dead sets up the action in a familiar way for Romero fans. We start out following a group of soldiers as they abandon their posts and take off on their own. There's a crossover here with the prior film: these are the soldiers who held up the protagonists in that film. They are led by a staff sergeant named Crockett.

The action quickly shifts to an Irish family feud, which is taking place off the coast of Delaware on picturesque Plum Island. The patriarchs of the two families, Patrick O'Flynn and Seamus Muldoon, lead the feud. They both have Irish accents and are well into middle age or their early elderly years.

The feud has erupted over how to deal with the dead. As far as O'Flynn is concerned, the dead need to be rounded up and killed off. Muldoon believes that they can be rehabilitated and, once the technology is developed, cured.

O'Flynn and his henchmen are exiled from the island by the dominant Muldoon clan, rather than being killed outright.

The soldiers meet up with Boy, who tells them about Plum Island and they head off to the ferry to get off the mainland and away from the dead. They end up having a gunfight with the O'Flynns. One of the soldiers manages to get control of one of the ferries. The living dead wipe out the O'Flynns. Patrick O'Flynn, however, manages to avoid death and joins up with the soldiers and heads back to the island.

The Muldoons have taken it upon themselves to star rehabilitating the zombies. They chain them up to keep them from biting anyone or from running off. The Muldoons teach them to live and work as they did when they were alive. Some of the soldiers decide to break off on their own but are quickly confronted by Muldoon men. One of them, Tomboy, survives and is taken back to the Muldoon compound, where she sees the zombies that the Muldoons have attempted to rehabilitate.

O'Flynn had twin daughters, Janet and Jane. Jane has been turned into a zombie and lives with the Muldoons. Janet decides to join up with her clan and to go after the Muldoon family. The O'Flynns end up surrendering to the Muldoons. Crockett has joined up with them and is also captured.

Zombie Jane is being taught to eat animal meat rather than human flesh. Janet tries to approach Zombie Jane but ends up getting bit, condemning Janet to being a zombie herself.

The zombies that the Muldoons had been, up until now, keeping under control are set loose. They descend upon the fighting parties and add to the overall body count. Eventually, Muldoon and O'Flynn agree to stop their war with one another. It lasts only a few minutes, however, and Muldoon shoots O'Flynn, who shoots Muldoon in retaliation, killing Muldoon.

O'Flynn holds on to life long enough to gun down Janet to prevent her from becoming a zombie, and then yells at the soldiers that he's proven himself a hard man by doing so.

The remaining soldiers, consisting of only Crockett and Tomboy, along with Boy, get back on the ferry and leave the island. A scene shows the zombies descending on a horse and eating the flesh, showing that Muldoon was, apparently, successful in teaching them to eat something other than human beings.

The final scene shows O'Flynn and Muldoon resurrected as zombies. Standing atop a hill against a full moon, they try to shoot one another with empty firearms. A voiceover muses about the pointlessness of the conflicts that consume humanity.

The Final Chapter, as of Now

There are remakes of Romero's *Dead* films in the works, but as of publication, this is the last new film that builds on Romero's universe that started with *Night of the Living Dead*. A ranking of this film in the earlier section that features Romero lists this as the weakest of the *Dead* films, which is only a matter of opinion, but one that is widely held.

The weaknesses in this film really don't have anything to do with Romero's directing or writing, which are still very strong. The world that started out with *NOTLD*, however, has been used as a staging ground for his stories since the late 1960s and, in this film, it's showing that there's really not much new ground to cover. This film combines the tension created by simply trying to survive the living dead with the tension created by the problems humanity as a whole deals with, even in the face of the zombie apocalypse. It's fertile ground for storytelling, but it's been harvested from several times before.

Like *Day of the Dead,* we have a mix of civilians and soldiers trying to make their way through an apocalyptic world. The soldiers, as is the case in the aforementioned film, have lost sight of their mission and, really, who can blame them? They're fighters without a war or a chain of command and, as such, they've taken to using their skills to survive as best they can, picking up a civilian in the form of Boy to add to their mix. It doesn't really matter what Boy's name is, which says something about the film.

Also in the vein of *Day of the Dead*, we have a group of civilians who are determined that the dead can be rehabilitated, which seems a reasonable goal since most of humanity seems to be shambling around and rotting away at this point. They tap those undead as a source of labor and try to teach them to be civilized, which has the flavor of a human-versus-nature plot. The dead are taking over the world bit by bit and, while Muldoon's scheme does seem to have some successful outcomes, it also seems like it's just delaying the inevitable.

What this film doesn't have that really drove the earlier films in this series, particularly the first two, is the feeling that the protagonists are in a state of utter terror and desperation in the face of the walking dead. In this film, the dead are more like cockroaches. They're a health threat if enough of them show up but, most of the time, they're just gross and easy to stomp out of existence. Crockett, at one point, actually lights one up with a flare gun and lights a cigarette off its head. It's funny and gives the film an interesting twist, but it also shows that the main sense of tension has largely been reduced to a slapstick threat. The characters seem to have an easier time dealing with the dead, for the most part, than hunters have dealing with wild boars or grizzly bears, both of which are intelligent, fast and deadly. The dead in this film really don't seem that threatening.

Overall, what this film shows is that the sense of urgency that defined the others has largely disappeared. Everyone knows that the living dead transmit the zombie plague by biting, so, as long as one keeps their body away from the zombies' mouths, they're fine. One does have to wonder why the Muldoons don't use the same strategy the North Koreans used in *28 Days Later* and just rip the teeth out of all the undead.

The soldiers in this film are out for themselves, but they're not nearly as sinister as the soldiers are in *28 Days Later*. They're more along the lines of people looking for something to do than traumatized killers just a few seconds away from killing or raping.

The family feud seems just plain odd. The idea of two men with heavy Irish accents battling it out on an island off the coast of Delaware seems like a stretch, even in a film where corpses eat horses. The ending has a social commentary element that fully fits in with Romero's other observations, as told through his films, but which is oddly heavy-handed for him. It's social commentary more along that seen in *Land of the Dead* than that seen in *Night of the Living Dead* or *Dawn of the Dead*.

Romero is still the master. This film does nothing to betray that legacy and it's still impossible not to respect him for managing to create a film antagonist with such rich possibilities. This film, however, shows a world that's petering out. It's petering out on-screen, as even the conflicts aren't that involving and, as the commentary itself indicates, people don't even know what they're fighting about. If they don't know why they're fighting, why should we care? Off the screen, it shows a universe that's really fading out out in terms of being able to hold audience interest. In today's ADD world, undead that take 10 minutes to make it across the lawn are just too slow for anyone to pay attention.

Enjoying These Zombies

In the world of zombie films, Romero's worst is still better than a lot of other directors' best. This film, in fact, is still better than the *Return of the Dead* series, which eventually got so silly that it was unwatchable. This film doesn't seem silly or trite, just tired.

Perhaps that fits well into this universe. The passage of time really seems to be foggy in Romero's films, which makes sense given that they're sometimes separated by decades and that more than 40 years have passed since the first one was released. The zombie apocalypse, by the time this film comes around, however, has become a sort of dull job. Wake up, shoot zombies, nail the door shut, go to sleep, wake up, shoot zombies, etc. It's routine and that comes off in the film. Even domesticating zombies has been explored before, so the idea that they can evolve isn't fresh at all.

There is some fun to be had in this film. As Roger Ebert pointed out, some very funny zombie kills in this film make it worth seeing. The plot between the feuding O'Flynn and Muldoon clan really doesn't add much to the film other than a motivation for gun fights. Basically, O'Flynn is a less-educated version of Frankenstein from *Day of the Dead* and the O'Flynn clan is the homicidal soldiers who seem like they'd be perfectly happy killing other human beings if there weren't so many zombies around to eat up their time and bullets.

The soldiers and the Boy in this story are avatars for the audience, seeing the feud from the outside and ending up involved in it, even if they only marginally care about it after a while. In the end, however, we're told by the narration itself that the entire thing has been utterly pointless and that no one really knows why they're fighting at all, whether that means fighting the endless swarms of undead or one another over disagreements that never needed to escalate to such a level of violence. Again, it begs the question, how can one be inspired by a film that feels so uninspired itself in most every regard? Watch it to complete the Romero zombie films, then watch *Night of the Living Dead, Dawn of the Dead,* and *Day of the Dead* to be reminded why Romero and his films are so important, because they are, even if this one really isn't.

Zombieland (2009)

Director:

Ruben Fleischer

Starring:

Jesse Eisenberg

Woody Harrelson

Emma Stone

Abigail Breslin

Zombieland is an enormously successful zombie comedy that surpassed the remake of *Dawn of the Dead* as the most financially successful zombie comedy of all time and held that title until 2013. It's fast-paced, darkly funny, and has great dialogue and special effects. Zombieland is intensely watchable.

The Plot

Zombieland doesn't reinvent the wheel where the zombie movie plots are concerned. There's been a zombie apocalypse and four people are trying to make it to family or to safe areas.

The characters are all named after cities that they're heading to. The main character, Columbus, is trying to make it back to Ohio. He was attending school in Austin, Texas, when the zombie plague hit. Before it happened, he was an extremely introverted sort, spending his time drinking soda and playing *World of Warcraft*. He has no close family or friends at the outset of the film, nor did he have any before the zombie apocalypse.

Woody Harrelson plays Tallahassee, a particularly gifted zombie slayer who's on his way east when he encounters Columbus. The two pair up and, though Harrelson is bristly at first, they quickly warm up to one another.

Tallahassee is obsessed with getting a Twinkie. He's also obsessed with killing zombies. While Columbus and anyone else who survived, presumably, has to kill zombies to survive, Tallahassee seems to have a particularly strong hatred for them. Early on, this is explained as a result of the zombies killing his puppy.

While the pair is looting a store, they meet Wichita and Little Rock. Wichita approaches the pair and tells them that her 12-year-old sister Little Rock has been bitten and is waiting to die. They've said their goodbyes already but they didn't have a gun. Wichita asks for a gun so she can shoot Little Rock, preventing her from becoming a zombie.

She gets a gun, and then turns it on Tallahassee and Columbus, demanding their vehicle and anything else they have.

Tallahassee and Columbus soon find a much better ride and plenty of guns and set off after the girls. They find them on the road and, once again, the girls scam them, but this time they take Tallahassee and Columbus with them, holding them at gunpoint.

Wichita and Little Rock want to go to Pacific Playland, an amusement park that they believe is free from zombies. After hearing that Columbus is a wasteland, Columbus—the man—agrees to go with them. Tallahassee decides to go, as well.

The group makes it to Hollywood and Tallahassee takes everyone to Bill Murray's mansion. It turns out that Bill Murray is still alive and has been moving among the zombies by using stage makeup to look undead himself. He, Harrelson, and Wichita have a good time of it. Murray decides to play a joke on Little Rock and Columbus, who don't know he is alive and are watching *Ghostbusters* in his theater. He and sneaks in dressed as a zombie. Columbus gets up and shoots Murray in the chest out of reflex.

The four spend the night together. Columbus figures out that Tallahassee has been saying he's enraged over the loss of his puppy, but he sees pictures in his wallet and figures out that Tallahassee actually lost his son. Tallahassee, however, starts to become something of a father figure to Little Rock.

Columbus and Wichita start to fall for one another. In the morning, however, she takes off for Pacific Playland with her sister, leaving Tallahassee and Columbus behind at Murray's mansion. They go after the girls once more.

The girls end up stuck on an amusement park ride with zombies gathered all around. Tallahassee and Columbus show up. Columbus goes to free Wichita and Little Rock, and Tallahassee has barricaded himself into a game stand and sets up a line of ammunition magazines. He's lured the zombies in and he begins cutting them down from the safety of the stand.

Columbus manages to get to Wichita and Little Rock and to get them down from the ride. Afterward, Tallahassee is raiding a concession stand for Twinkies when, thinking there's a zombie behind the door, Columbus shoots into a storage locker and destroys a box of Twinkies that Tallahassee then finds on the shelf. Little Rock gives him one and the four all take off together. Columbus realizes that, for the first time in his life, he has something resembling a real family.

Witty and Grown-Up

To its credit *Zombieland* lacks a lot of the silly slapstick and high school-level jokes that you'll find in some other zombie comedies,. It's just as good as *Shaun of the Dead*, though very different.

This film manages to be funny, dark and lighthearted all at the same time. There isn't any really serious depth to the character's relationships, but the performances are so good all around that it's believable that they're all growing to like one another.

The dialogue in this film is great and Woody Harrelson and Jesse Eisenberg get a real rhythm going with how they talk to one another. This is one of those films where it's not hard at all to listen to the characters talk. They don't go on self-indulgent monologues, their jokes aren't strained and their timing is very good. When Wichita and Little Rock show up, it just gets better and none of the characters is one that the audience will be secretly hoping is killed off.

Bill Murray is in fine form here, as well. Tallahassee practically worships the man. Little Rock doesn't know who he is, which is why she ends up watching *Ghostbusters* with Columbus. By the time the characters get to the mansion, they have an obvious attachment to one another, which actually makes this an even better film than it had to be. It would have been funny enough, but the actors and the script allow the audience to grow attached to the characters. By the time everyone's at Pacific Playground for the final confrontation, most anyone who's watched the movie to that point will be invested in all the characters.

This is a very witty film and a lot of the wit is exhibited in how it handles zombie film clichés. What it does very well is have fun with those clichés without really disparaging them in any way, which would have been easier to write, for certain, but not nearly as funny.

A Great and Funny Guide to Surviving the Zombie Apocalypse

Some movies are self-aware and pull that off to great effect. *Scream* is a prime example. This film is another.

Columbus has come up with a set of very sensible rules that he follows to stay alive. They include practical advice, such as putting on your seatbelt, and advice that's born from his experiences surviving the zombie apocalypse, such as being wary in bathrooms, where zombies seem to know people are vulnerable.

Some of his other rules are clear references to horror and zombie film clichés. For instance, the "Double Tap" rule involves putting an extra round in anything you kill, just to be sure, because they always get up when you don't. He also strongly advises cardio fitness and, early in the film, actually gives a pretty impressive demonstration of how he uses that to survive. He even limbers up before doing anything strenuous, because cramping up can actually be fatal in a bad situation.

Columbus is a nerd and an introvert and the movie has a good time with showing how he, for the most part, seems comfortable with the zombie apocalypse. He wants to go find his parents, but he doesn't seem to be losing his mind with loneliness by any measure. His incessant rulemaking and adherence to them keeps him alive and makes him a great foil for Tallahassee.

Tallahassee is another zombie movie cliché who's rendered in a very fun way in this film. He's the all-around badass. He uses weapons like pruning shears, banjos and just about anything else and, in his hands, any of them can quickly and easily dispatch a zombie. Harrelson pulls this character off brilliantly.

Wichita is a great con artist and is very loyal and protective of her sister. She's basically the vixen and the mother character in one and she's very likeable, even when she's running her scams. Stone plays her very well and she never makes her unlikeable. Little Rock is very similar to her. Where zombie films are full of screaming, frightened children, Little Rock is really quite tough and dependable. At one point, she blames it on violent video games.

This film has just about every zombie movie cliché within its runtime and has great fun with all of them. There's one more cliché that's really played to great effect.

Columbus is terrified of clowns. Even in the middle of the zombie apocalypse, he has horrifying visions of clowns. How he faces up to this at the end is really quite brilliant and used as a very funny moment of catharsis.

There are quite a few Easter egg references to other films scattered throughout this one, so be sure to watch it a couple of times if you like finding them.

Enjoying These Zombies

The zombies in *Zombieland* are basically the all-terrain tires of the zombie apocalypse. They're not so slow that they're shamblers, and they're not so fast that they're of the same threat level as the zombies in *28 Days Later*. They're as fast as the plot needs them to be and, for the most part, they're just there to kill. There's even a zombie kill-of-the-week thing going on between Tallahassee and Columbus, with a particularly good, and cartoonish one featured during the film.

The zombies in this film are generally stupid and unsympathetic. They're on the same level in this film that they are in video games—violent video games, as Little Rock notes.

What's fun about the zombies in this movie is how they act as foils. They bring out the beast in Tallahassee and Woody Harrelson is athletic and big enough to be very intimidating. It's believable that he could off a zombie with a banjo, or most anything else. The zombie apocalypse gets Columbus out of his room for once and it makes Wichita and Little Rock more honest.

The writers here gave just enough background for each of the characters for us to care that they make it through the zombies they encounter and that they stick together. That makes it possible for them to be very funny, as well.

Zombieland and *Shaun of the Dead* are probably the best zombie comedies out there. As mentioned ealier, they've very different, but both very funny in their own ways.

As one last endorsement, this film has an incredible 90% rating from critics on Rotten Tomatoes. It's that good.

World War Z (2013)

Director:

Marc Forster

Starring:

Brad Pitt

Mireille Enos

Matthew Fox

This is a big-budget film based on the book of the same name by Max Brooks. It got good reviews and does a lot with the money that was spent on its production. In this film, we're given a familiar version of the zombie apocalypse story that still manages to stay interesting, despite it being very conventional at times.

The Plot

Pitt plays Gerry Lane. He used to work for the UN as an investigator, but gave it up after the stress of the job took its toll on him and because he wanted to spend more time with his family. One morning while he and his family are driving in downtown Philadelphia, the world changes forever.

A zombie attack begins when they're in traffic, but by the time it hits Philadelphia, it's already been ravaging cities across the world. The dead in this film are turned into plague-crazed zombies within seconds of being bit, so the infection rages through the traffic jam right in front of the character's eyes.

Lane has worked in dangerous places, and he manages to get his family out of the city. He's friends with the Deputy Secretary of the UN, Umutoni, and calls him for assistance. Umutoni needs Lane to help investigate the plague and agrees to send a helicopter when Lane can find an extraction point.

The family heads to Newark, which is already devastated. Lane's daughter has asthma and they go to get her medication for it at a pharmacy. The drug store is completely overrun and Lane's wife, Karin, is nearly raped by two men in the store before Lane kills one of them and chases the other one off with a deer rifle.

Lane and his family leave the store to find their vehicle stolen. They take off to a nearby apartment building where they hunker down for the night with a family who's determined not to leave. The next morning, zombies flood the building as Lane and his family flee. The take the son of the family from the apartment building with them and are evacuated to an aircraft carrier in the Atlantic. The UN is operating from it and a group of other ships that have taken shelter from the plague offshore.

Lane doesn't want to be part of the investigation to find the cause of the plague, but is persuaded to agree when the commander of the carrier group lets Lane know that Lane and his whole family will be sent back to Philadelphia if he doesn't help.

Lane is teamed up with a genius virologist and a group of Navy SEALs, who want to find the first infected person to determine a vaccine for the virus. They are sent to South Korea where the first known case of the virus occurred at a military base.

The virologist accidentally kills himself, leaving Lane in charge of the mission on the ground. The soldiers at the base explain that the virus apparently came from their own doctor. The virus spread through several other people at the base before the soldiers contained and incinerated the infected. The infected happened to have ignored one soldier, who has a bad leg.

Lane finds out from a former CIA agent that the North Koreans have been weathering the plague well, after having removed everyone's teeth to prevent the plague from spreading, as bites are the most common vectors for the infection. He also finds out that the Israelis were ready for the plague and that he should seek out a Mossad officer named Jurgen Warmbrunn.

The zombies overrun the base while Gerry and the people he's with make it back to their plane to head to Israel. He's allowed to land in Jerusalem, which is surrounded by high walls.

When he talks to Warmbrunn, he finds out that the Israelis had, after enduring many hardships, decided to institute a policy called the "10th man". The idea is that, if nine of their leaders agree on something, the tenth must disagree and act accordingly. The Israelis had received intelligence that the Indian army was fighting rakshasa, their word for undead. Being the 10th man, Warmbrunn worked under the assumption that "undead" meant exactly what it meant and that he needed to prepare Israel for a zombie attack. He did, and the city is surviving when Gerry arrives.

When people make it into the walls, the other survivors greet them with songs and shouts. Unfortunately, this attracts the attention of the zombies outside the walls. They begin climbing up on one another, reaching the top of the wall and attacking en masse. While Gerry is trying to get out with the help of the Israeli soldiers, he notices that the zombies run right by some people without giving them a second look, just as they ignored the lame soldier in Korea.

Gerry manages to escape, along with an Israeli commando. The commando is bitten on the way out, but by amputating her arm before the virus spreads from the bite, Gerry is able to save her.

The two manage to get a message from the Deputy Secretary of the UN to the pilot of the aircraft they get out on. The aircraft is given clearance to land near a WHO research facility in the UK, where Gerry can get assistance.

While they're on board, a stowaway zombie infects a crewmember. The infection spreads through one half of the airplane in minutes. The other passengers try to build a barrier, but the zombies start pouring over it. Gerry takes a grenade from the commando and, after her sidearm runs out of ammo, he throws it into the back of the plane, blasting a hole in the hull. The zombies fall out of the plane, which manages to make an emergency landing.

Gerry and the commando survive and make it to the WHO facility. After he persuades the people at the facility who he is, he starts telling them his theory. He believes that the zombies avoid anyone who's ill or unhealthy. The virus is getting them to spread the disease to other hosts, but they're only interested hosts who seem healthy and likely to survive.

Gerry's idea is that they let loose an infection, and the zombies will ignore anyone who carries it. If the infection is a curable one, Gerry reasons, they could use it as a way to camouflage themselves against the zombies and then get treatment for the infection before it kills them.

The facility has plenty of infectious diseases, but it requires that Gerry make his way through a part of the facility that's been overrun with zombies. He, the commando, and the head of the facility go in to get the infection.

Segen, the commando, and the head of the facility all get chased out by the zombies. Gerry manages to get into the freezer where they keep the infectious diseases. He grabs a container full of samples, but gets cornered by one of the zombies. Taking a chance, he infects himself with one of the samples and waits a while for it to kick in. He then exits the freezer and the zombie completely ignores him after determining that he's ill. Gerry manages to walk through the remaining zombies and to get back to the doctors, who treat him for the disease with which he injected himself.

The film ends showing Gerry returning to his family, who have been evacuated to a safe area in Nova Scotia. The plan Gerry devised has resulted in the creation of a vaccine that allows the living to avoid being attacked by the zombies. It's distributed around the world. He makes it clear that the war hasn't ended, however.

Familiar, but Fun, Zombies

The zombies in this film are of the fast, infected variety we see in *28 Days Later*. In fact, that's not where the similarities between this film and that one end. The presumed virus that the zombies are spreading is referred to as "rabies" at one point. It's not given a formal name and it's not really described, which makes sense, given that this film follows Gerry and he's an investigator, not a virologist. He does his best to find a way to survive the zombies, and does, but his medical knowledge is limited.

The zombies in this film behave almost like colony insects. When they need to reach a height inaccessible to one of them, they start piling up and climbing on one another to make it accessible. They seem to have no regard for their own wellbeing, just as is the case with many other film zombies. They dive headfirst off heights and into cars, and get right up, running down anyone in their paths.

The zombie plague spreads much like the Rage virus in *28 Days Later* in that it takes less than a minute for it to overwhelm the victim's body and turn them into a zombie. The infected in this film aren't as gruesome as they are in *28 Days Later,* where they spat blood almost constantly. In this film, however, they're gruesome enough and it's their savagery and their speed that make them frightening.

The zombies in this film aren't anything new. They don't really add anything to the canon, and in many regards, the film relies on what we already know to weave an interesting tale. Everyone knows that zombie bites can spread the plague and everyone knows it's probably a virus and, conceivably, there could be a vaccine. These are well-developed tropes in zombie films and this film seems to realize that it can still be entertaining without reinventing the wheel, so to speak. It does call the zombies "zekes," which is a popular trope these days. In the game *Killing Floor*, for example, the zombies are called zeds. In the same way that we know that the plague is spread by viruses, we understand that "zeke" is another derivative of zombie, like "z."

This is another convention in films, one that's called "Our Zombies Are Different" by TV Tropes. Essentially, these zombies take the massive assault of Romero's zombies and combine it with the plague zombie to create a creature that's old and new at the same time. It works, however, and the filmmakers did a great job of putting the action shots together. The scenes where the zombies are shown to be so crazed that they'll run right off a building after a helicopter are particularly memorable and tense.

The zombies in this film are somewhat intelligent. They're at least smart enough to know the difference between a good and a bad host. Other than that, they seem largely dimwitted. They cannot operate doors nor do anything else so complex. They don't attack one another, however, indicating that the virus also recognizes other infected just as it does unsuitable hosts, or at least it makes the host recognize as much.

What Is Different

In this film, Gerry's brains really save the day. He's not a fast-shooting, machete-swinging badass. He's more of an intellectual badass. The film is something of a procedural, showing the process that Gerry goes through to figure out the weakness of the virus. He takes information from the virologist who accidently kills himself and combines it with his own observations to arrive at a testable hypothesis. Having that hypothesis, he volunteers himself as the first test subject—out of necessity—and confirms it. The film, even though it has a ton of action, has a great science element to it that makes it interesting beyond the character just trying to survive.

Because Gerry is not just trying to survive, the story has other interesting twists. One can easily imagine the other passengers on the airliner that Gerry takes out of Israel getting home to Belarus, grabbing their shotguns, food, and water and heading for the hills. That's what people do in most zombie films. In this film, Gerry is one of the people who are trying to stop the zombie apocalypse, as opposed to merely surviving it, and that gives it an interesting element, as well.

Gerry actually ends up being a lot of fun as a protagonist. The story gives him something more substantial to figure out than how to find food, water or shelter. The plot unfolds at a very fast pace. Despite the fact that this is unabashedly a zombie film—the use of the words "zeke" and "rakshasa" just adds color—it doesn't overuse its zombies. The story isn't afraid to let them just be a menace once in a while rather than having them chase Gerry and company around constantly, which makes it more dramatic when they do make an appearance.

Enjoying These Zombies

One of the real joys of *World War Z* is that it was shot with such a high budget. The shots of the first zombie attacks, while Gerry and his family are stuck in traffic, are very effective. There is certainly no shortage of car chases in today's films, but this one is done well enough to make it believable. The filmmakers also opted to avoid going for over-the-top hysterics from the child characters, such as Dakota Fanning's shrieking in Steven Spielberg's *War of the Worlds*. The kids lose it here, as would anyone, but it's convincing how the family comes together and they all prove to have enough competence to survive. Brad Pitt gets an interesting character in that he's clearly experienced with dangerous places and knows how to handle himself, but he's not a commando who can go blasting through adversaries willy-nilly and be relatively certain he'll survive.

The zombie attacks are excellent. The zombies in this film are fast-moving predators, just as they are in *28 Days Later*, but their wildness is even more extreme in this film. When they attack, there's just no time to do anything but run and the plague spreads so quickly that there really isn't any chance of stopping it before it claims a great number of people.

World War Z is well worth watching. The high budget of this film shows how popular and profitable zombie films have become. There's no firm indication as of yet that there will be a sequel, even though the closing implies strongly that there will be. Even without a sequel, this film is worth seeing and a good example of zombie horror in the 21st century.

http://tvtropes.org/pmwiki/pmwiki.php/Main/OurZombiesAreDifferent

Further Recommendations

The films that follow vary in terms of quality. For true fans of zombie cinema, there may be some good times to be had in this list. They are not, however, on the caliber of the other zombie films featured in this book, so be aware that you might spend a bit of time groaning, as if you yourself had just crawled out of the grave. Some of these films would clearly benefit from more brains.

The Astro Zombies (1968)

This film is a completely unintelligible cult classic. Its most redeeming qualities are the ultra-low production, the over-the-top performances, plot holes you could drive a Mac truck through and the presence of Tura Satana, a Chinese spy working with Mexican spies, for some reason. The plot involves Dr. Demarco's mad quest to create robot zombie space pilots. Of course, it all goes horribly wrong and murder ensures. This film has become legendary for how bad it really is and, if you like movies that are so bad they're good, this one will likely stay with you. It opens up with a shot of toy wind-up robots, so you get an idea of what kind of movie you're watching right away. A must-see for fans of B-movies.

Zombie Holocaust (1979)

This film was released under the tile *Zombie 3* and is Italian, but is not a Fulci zombie film. The action takes place in New York City, where cannibalism has been discovered. Investigators find that hospitals where immigrants from the Maluki Islands have been working have reported similar incidents. In addition to cannibals, the action soon involves zombies of the Vodou style, as well, resulting in a lot of gore and carnage.

City of the Dead (1980)

Fulci returns with this zombie-themed film that belongs to what some consider a trilogy of films, including *The Beyond* and *The House by the Cemetery*. The zombies in this film are far more powerful than they're usually depicted as being in other films and they come right from Hell. The film has a Lovecraft connection in that the characters have to go to Dunwich to end the zombie plague.

Zombie High (1987)

This film centers on a plot that involves the faculty stealing brain matter from the students and using mind control to keep them in line. The film is very low-budget and the effects are, at times, hilarious. It's intended to be something of a zombie comedy, but falls short of the mark of *Return of the Living Dead* and doesn't even get close to brilliant films like *Shaun of the Dead* and *Zombieland*.

Return of the Living Dead Part II (1988)

If you liked the first *Return of the Living Dead*, you'll likely enjoy the second installment. If the first was too silly for you, you most certainly will not. This film takes the spontaneous humor of the first and ratchets it up a few levels. The zombies in this film are more comedic than menacing, particularly one that looks like Michael Jackson. It does have some slapstick gore here and there and, for those who like silly humor and zombies, it might be a great film to consider looking at.

Chopper Chicks in Zombietown (1989)

If you're a fan of the bizarre and quirky, two names associated with this film will likely catch your interest right away: Billy Bob Thornton and Troma, the company behind such films as *The Toxic Avenger*. This film follows the all female club, Cycle Sluts MC, as they roll into Zariah looking for some hell to raise. The town is ruled by a mad scientist who makes zombies work in a mine, but they end up getting loose and terrorizing the town. The Cycle Sluts ride into action, fighting the zombie and eventually taking them all out, saving the town and becoming heroines. It's a Troma film, so one should be relatively certain of what they're getting, and, of course, the film delivers on that.

Pet Semetary (1989)

Based on the Stephen King book of the same name, this film isn't a true zombie film, but it does involve the dead rising from the grave. In fact, it's a lot more frightening and supernatural than most of the zombie films out there, so you'll want to look if you're in want of something with zombie themes but that's more serious than most of the zombie films from this era. These zombies don't eat your brain, but they're about as evil as anything can be and the film is quite effective.

Bride of Re-Animator (1990)

If you thought Herbert West was done for at the end of the first *Re-Animator*, you were wrong. He returns in this second installment of the series, which, again, follows Lovecraft's story, at least for the most part. The film takes place in South America, where the doctors can work their wonders on the freshly dead. When they come back home, they can't give it up. Not only do we get a second installment featuring the two main characters form the first film, but Dr. Hill also returns in this film, though again, he's just a head, at least until he figures out how to use those mind control powers we saw him use in the first film to greater effect!

Beyond Re-Animator (2003)

Right on time to cash in on the new zombie craze, Herbert West makes a return to the screen. This time, he's in prison and conducting his experiments with limited resources. He finds a helper in Howard Phillips—H.P. Lovecraft's first and middle names—and soon is able to resume his mad enterprise. This film considers what happens when you can no longer tell the living from the dead and, as far as West is concerned, how far madness will propel one. It's a fun third installment for people who love this series.

Zombie Strippers (2008)

Zombie Strippers is a zom com that leaves little doubt as to what the film centers on. It stars two fixtures of their respective genres. Robert Englund, horror legend and famous for playing Freddy Krueger, teams up with Jenna Jameson, famous adult film star, for this film. The comedy centers on how the strippers at Englund's club actually become more popular after they've been zombified. The film features a lot of gross-out and crude humor and, for those who live for that sort of thing and who love zombies, it should be enjoyable. It's definitely not on the level of the best zombie comedies out there, however.

Tokyo Zombie (2009)

Japan produces no shortage of gore films and zombie films oftentimes fall under that category. This film is adapted from a manga book of the same name. Like many other Japanese stories, this one deals with the unintended consequences of polluting the environment—making zombies, in this case—and features some martial arts heroes.

Conclusion

When one looks at zombie films overall, it's obvious that there are two distinct mythologies that they draw upon, and occasionally blend. The Vodou zombie is really the zombie of the past but, sometimes, a great film such as *The Serpent and the Rainbow* manages to make them frightening, and current, once more. For the most part, however, we're in the age of the zombie horde.

Today's zombies are sometimes target practice, sometimes rabid animals, and sometimes social commentary. Zombies can be more sympathetic and likeable than one may have ever imagined when *Night of the Living Dead* came out, or they can be far more horrific and violent.

As the appetite for these films grew in the 2000s, the way that the zombies were portrayed started to embrace both fast and slow zombies. Both of them are currently featured in popular films and television shows, as well as in video games.

No matter how fast they moved, in other words, zombies have spread. They've gone from folk tales and religious stories to Vodou zombie movies. They gradually expanded from film into television and books. From there, they banged on the doors of the video game industry and, when they first made a memorable appearance in a game, they revitalized the zombie film as a viable product.

Right now, it seems like zombie films are poised to keep on delivering at the box office. As long as creative directors and writers can come up with new ways to feature them, there's no reason that they shouldn't remain commercially viable.

Even if they don't remain commercially viable, however, it's no reason to despair. Even in the days when zombies were largely B-movie fare, some of the best of the zombie movies came out and, in fact, the most legendary of all, *Night of the Living Dead*, was a low-budget film. These creatures, fortunately for low-budget filmmakers, don't require expensive special effects or exotic settings to work. All one needs are a few reanimated dead, a good set for the characters to fight them off on, and a decent story. The proof is in some of the films in this book and in many others that are out there waiting to be explored.

Like the creatures they feature, these films keep rising up over and over again, and they seem to be coming in an unstoppable wave. Fortunately, it's the public devouring the zombies, and not the other way around.

Sources Cited

http://www.rogerebert.com/reviews/the-night-of-the-living-dead-1968

http://www.livescience.com/23892-zombies-real-facts.html

http://www.bbc.com/culture/story/20131025-zombie-nation

http://tvtropes.org/pmwiki/pmwiki.php/Film/Plan9FromOuterSpace.

http://www.openculture.com/2013/12/plan-9-from-outer-space.html

http://forrestcrow.proboards.com/thread/6893

https://www.youtube.com/watch?v=l5DZhDH8eew

https://www.youtube.com/watch?v=drMczeQYIBg

http://www.imdb.com/title/tt0063350/trivia?ref_=ttspec_ql_trv_1

http://www.merriam-webster.com/dictionary/ghoul

http://www.plagiarismtoday.com/2011/10/10/how-a-copyright-mistake-created-the-modern-zombie/

https://archive.org/details/night_of_the_living_dead

http://www.youtube.com/watch?v=AvA4NNqx7Os

http://www.dagonbytes.com/thelibrary/lovecraft/reanimator.htm

http://www.americanpopularculture.com/journal/articles/fall_2002/harper.htm

http://zombie.wikia.com/wiki/Dawn_of_the_Dead_(ZOMBI_1978)

http://zombie.wikia.com/wiki/Differences_Between_Surviving_Fast_and_Slow_Zombies

http://www.ejumpcut.org/archive/onlinessays/JC28folder/WhiteZombie.html

https://www.youtube.com/watch?v=WFLjN-BNS1Y

http://zombie.wikia.com/wiki/T-Virus

http://www.gamefront.com/5-things-you-might-not-know-about-the-resident-evil-films/

http://tvtropes.org/pmwiki/pmwiki.php/Main/ConservationOfNinjutsu

http://www.selfdevelopment.net/hypnosis/HypnosisHypnotism/Stage-Hypnosis-What-is-it-and-How-to-do-it

http://www.runnersworld.com/weight-loss/how-many-calories-are-you-really-burning

http://www.cracked.com/article_18683_7-scientific-reasons-zombie-outbreak-would-fail-quickly_p4.html

http://www.slate.com/articles/arts/culturebox/2004/03/dead_run.html

http://www.nlm.nih.gov/medlineplus/ency/article/007192.htm

http://www.rottentomatoes.com/m/28_days_later/

http://health.yodelout.com/contagious-diseases-human-disease-spreaders-carriers/

http://www.aintitcool.com/node/35671

http://screenrant.com/day-of-the-dead-remake-2014/

http://www.rottentomatoes.com/m/survival_of_the_dead/

http://www.rogerebert.com/reviews/survival-of-the-dead-2010

http://tvtropes.org/pmwiki/pmwiki.php/Main/LawfulEvil

http://www.rottentomatoes.com/m/zombieland/

http://www.americanpopularculture.com/journal/articles/fall_2002/harper.htm

http://www.cerebration.org/adrianversteegh.html

http://www.academia.edu/2076353/Locating_Zombies_in_the_Sociology_of_Popular_Culture

http://songmeanings.com/songs/view/3530822107858607660/

http://web.archive.org/web/20070216005517/http://www.diamonddead.com/diary/view.php?s=YToyOntzOjM6ImFpZCI7czoxOiIzIjtzOjI6ImlkIjtzOjI6IjI4Ijt9

http://www.rottentomatoes.com/m/serpent_and_the_rainbow/

http://mancunion.com/2013/03/20/why-do-we-love-zombie-flicks/

http://books.google.com/books?id=VJ1vcmaOd7wC&pg=PA17&lpg=PA17&dq=censorship,+violent+films,+1980s&source=bl&ots=3C7VM4PZTc&sig=Sq5iQUxv-YXorMIFWV7T9f9UWNg&hl=en&sa=X&ei=uREzU52JH4SWqwHJ8YDgBA&ved=0CEQQ6AEwBA#v=onepage&q=censorship%2C%20violent%20films%2C%201980s&f=false

https://www.youtube.com/watch?v=NX-2O2n3DIs

http://web.archive.org/web/20050428004220/http://65.127.124.62/south_asia/4483241.stm.htm

http://www.snopes.com/humor/iftrue/zombies.asp

http://www.reuters.com/article/2013/02/12/us-usa-zombie-montana-idUSBRE91B1IA20130212

http://www.cdc.gov/phpr/images/Zombie_Poster_highres.pdf

http://www.foxnews.com/tech/2012/06/03/scammers-hope-youll-bite-on-zombie-news/

http://whatculture.com/film/10-reasons-why-dawn-of-the-dead-remake-sucks.php/2

www.ingramcontent.com/pod-product-compliance
Lightning Source LLC
LaVergne TN
LVHW051823080426
835512LV00018B/2706